GEORGE FOX

NEW APPRECIATIONS

OF

GEORGE FOX

A TERCENTENARY COLLECTION OF STUDIES

FOREWORD BY

J. RENDEL HARRIS, LL.D.

KENNIKAT PRESS
Port Washington, N. Y./London

NEW APPRECIATIONS OF GEORGE FOX

First published in 1925
Reissued in 1971 by Kennikat Press
Library of Congress Catalog Card No: 78-118539
ISBN 0-8046-1163-7

Manufactured by Taylor Publishing Company   Dallas, Texas

EDITORIAL NOTE

THE editors take this opportunity of thanking all those, authors and editors, who have so kindly given permission for the reprinting of the articles collected in this volume.

CONTENTS

GEORGE FOX

FOREWORD

By Dr. J. Rendel Harris.

Every centenary of the great man or the great movement, whether a plain centenary, a bi-centenary, a ter-centenary (as here), or an nth-centenary, is, as Browning would say, " a spark that disturbs our clod." It raises the question as to why we should remember, and, the deeper question, what right have we to forget. Yet it must be admitted that, in responding to the challenge, one is likely to be the subject of an uneasy suspicion as to whether we may not be found defaulters under the statute against whitewashing the tombs of the prophets and other closely related religious unrealities. In the present little volume I hope we are free from the condemnation in question (one of the severer oracles of the Master) ; for certainly George Fox was a real prophet, and those who speak of him with retrospective affection in the following pages are not of the Pharisaic brood. They will not, we think, have to face an entry in their spiritual audit in the form

To whitewashing the statue of George Fox, one coin of merit.

It is my happiness to know them all, with the exception of the Editor of the *Spectator* (upon

9

whom be peace ! He shall be judged by the company into which he has projected himself). Not a man of them would take part in a procession for the sake of waving a favourite flag, nor engage in a celebration with the object of provoking personal adulation by reflection from the glittering merits of another. Wherefore it is a goodly and a gracious exercise to listen to what they have to say about the man who, in his own day, recalled men from the circumference of religion to the centre, and from the perplexity of religious thought and the complexity of religious duty to the Grace which is within, where Christ affirmed that the Kingdom of God would be found : to wit, Righteousness, Peace and Joy in the Holy Ghost.

GEORGE FOX

THE LIFE OF GEORGE FOX IN OUTLINE

By T. Edmund Harvey, M.A.

It is one of the ironic revenges of history that in 1924 men should be celebrating the tercentenary of the birth of a man who did not believe in the celebration of anniversaries and would not have wished his name to be singled out in this way. George Fox is one of the very few religious leaders of the modern world chosen by Auguste Comte for a place in the Positivist Calendar, because his life and teaching were felt by the great French thinker to have a deep significance for humanity. He was the son of a Puritan Leicestershire weaver, whose neighbours called him " righteous Christer." At one time his relatives proposed that the grave lad should be trained for the priesthood in the Established Church, " but others," he tells us, " persuaded to the contrary." Simply educated and apprenticed to a shoemaker, who was also a grazier, Fox had the advantage of a mother, Mary

Lago, " accomplished " (as Penn tells us) " above most of her degree " in her neighbourhood, who understood his thoughtful, serious bent. Tending his sheep alone, he had time to meditate as he sought for a way of life which should be honest to God and man.

In 1643 came an unexpected turning-point in his life. He was asked by a cousin and another acquaintance, a professing Christian, to share a jug of beer with them in a tavern, and then pressed to spend the evening drinking toasts. He refused to stay, going home with a sad heart. He had realized the unreality of conventional religion, and after a sleepless night went away from his family and friends in search of the truth he longed for. For four years he wandered, seeking help in vain from teachers and preachers, whether among the Puritan clergy of the Established Church or the Dissenters, whom he found " more tender," yet still unable to meet his need. The help he sought came at length from no outside teacher, but in the silence of his own soul. Alone with his Bible in solitary places he passed much of his time, often, too, walking and meditating by night. Sometimes gleams of light came, in which he saw that all true Christians are passed from death into life, and that college education was not enough to qualify for the ministry. Perhaps he had felt depressed, as the stirrings of his great call first came to him, because he had not been given the training which was needful. This new thought came to him as an " opening from the Lord." But still he had to go through deep searchings of spirit. He sought in vain for help from others. At length, he tells us, when all his hopes in men were gone, and he knew not what to do, " then, oh ! then, I heard a voice which said, ' There is one, even Christ Jesus, that can speak to thy condition ' ; and when I heard it, my heart did leap for joy."

He had yet to go through deep waters, but from that time onward the sense of the presence of the Light of Christ in his heart grew stronger and became the inspiring strength of his life and ministry. He began, as he went to and fro, to endeavour to turn others to the same inward Teacher. The message came to him : " That which people trample upon must be thy food." He felt that people fed upon words and trampled upon the life. At the outset of his ministry he sometimes had to pass through inward gloom and trial, but it was after such a time that he wrote : " I saw also that there was an ocean of darkness and death ; but an infinite ocean of light and love, which flowed over the ocean of darkness."

He passed to and fro amid the later stages of the Civil War with no thought, it seems, for anything but his mission. Yet he was not living apart from the social needs of the time, for in 1648 we find him appealing at the statute hirings and in fairs and markets for just wages for servants and against oppression, and the plea thus begun was carried out throughout his life in steadfastly pressing for a

simple way of living, for fair dealing, fixed prices in
trade (unknown at that day, when Friends made it
their practice) and for just and brotherly relations
between master and man.

It was in this year that, as he writes, " the Lord
God opened to me by His invisible power that
every man was enlightened by the Divine Light of
Christ ; and I saw it shine through all ; and that
they that believed in it came out of condemnation
to the light of life, and became the children of it ;
but they that hated it and did not believe in it
were condemned by it, though they made a confession of Christ. This I saw in the pure openings
of the light, without the help of any man ; neither
did I then know where to find it in the Scriptures,
though afterwards, searching the Scriptures, I found
it." This became the keynote of all his subsequent
message, which was to " direct people to the Spirit,
that gave forth the Scriptures." It was a gospel
of inward experience, making its appeal, not by
intellectual argument, but by seeking to reach the
Divine witness in the heart and conscience of the
hearers ; for at the centre of George Fox's message
lay the conviction that the Divine Light shone into
every human life, that all might respond to it.

At the outset he felt required to avoid the forms
of customary civility, " without any respect to rich
or poor, great or small." His refusal to doff his
hat or use the courtly " you " to the great in place
of the familiar " thou " caused him constant
trouble ; but he never wavered in maintaining a

protest, which in its essence was one for truthfulness and for the equal human rights of all men in the sight of God.

Already here and there in the Midlands groups of those in sympathy with his teaching began to meet together for worship. In the organized forms of religion he had found no help for his own need, and he felt that he was to bring men away from their unreality " to the Church in God." In 1649, at Nottingham, he was imprisoned for the first time as a result of the impetuous message of protest with which he had actually interrupted the sermon of the minister in the great church. It was not the Scriptures, but the Holy Spirit which inspired them, he pleaded, that was the test by which doctrines, religions, and judgments were to be tried.

Often during the days of the Commonwealth, when the " liberty of prophesying " permitted such a practice, he followed the preacher by a sermon of a very different sort, but this seems to have been the only occasion when he actually interrupted the preacher in his sermon.

On his release Fox continued his travels, preaching at fairs and in churches ; sometimes beaten and stoned by the angry mob, at others meeting with a better response. He tells us of one or two remarkable cases where healing of mind and body followed his ministration at this time. At intervals throughout his *Journal* there are similar instances of this gift, which he records but does not seek to explain. From contemporary accounts we must picture him as large of frame, with long, straight locks of hair (not close-cropped, as was the Puritan custom), and with singularly penetrating eyes, which more than once daunted those who were about to attack him. For convenience of travel he wore leather breeches and a leather jerkin. The report would spread, as he reached a new district, " The man in leather breeches is come."

In 1650 came Fox's first long imprisonment ; he was accused of blasphemy for speaking at the close of a preaching service in Derby Church. It was here that the nickname of Quaker was first jestingly given him by one of the magistrates. He spent a year in Derby Gaol, though after a while he was allowed to walk a mile's distance from his prison, and made use of this liberty to speak occasionally in the market-place as well as to attend meetings. So great was the impression he made that, when soldiers were being raised to meet the Royalist Army from Scotland before the battle of Worcester, the Commonwealth Commissioners offered, at the soldiers' demand, to give Fox a captaincy. Fox made answer that he knew whence wars and fightings came, and that he " lived in the virtue of that life and power that took away the occasion of all wars." He steadfastly refused their offer, and in punishment was committed for months to the filthy felons' dungeon, which he shared with thirty felons, without any bed. Here he was able to comfort some poor thieves, who suffered capital punishment under the cruel laws of those days, and he wrote from his prison to protest against the iniquity of such harsh laws.

In 1651 he was set free and held meetings in his own home county of Leicestershire, and a little later went northward to Yorkshire, where James Naylor and William Dewsbury, afterwards leading Quaker ministers, came to hear him and were convinced. He travelled through the North and East Ridings, spreading his message of the " true Teacher within," and in 1652 passed over the Lancashire border and climbed to the top of Pendle Hill, where, he tells us, the Lord let him " see in what places he had a great people to be gathered."

Close by, in the northern corner of Yorkshire, in Furness, and in Westmorland, he did indeed find a great company of men and women prepared to join with whole-hearted enthusiasm in the new fellowship of " Friends of Truth " or "Children of the Light," as the early Quakers first called themselves. For some time before in this district groups of Seekers had been meeting together, having failed to find the help they needed in any existing sect. Fox's message thus fell on prepared ground, and from this hill-country of the North a large group of Quaker preachers, several of whom had previously been Puritan ministers of esteem, went forth to other parts of England to bring the message of vital Christianity, not found in books or discovered by argument, but making its appeal to the ever-present witness of God at work in every heart. The home of Judge Fell at

Swarthmore Hall, near Ulverstone, became the centre of this mission, the Judge, at first critical of Fox and his friends, showing extraordinary tolerance and increasing sympathy as time passed. On Fox's first visit to Swarthmore the Judge was absent on circuit. Fox, with the permission of the clergyman, spoke to the congregation in Ulverstone Church. "What have any to do with the Scriptures, but as they come to the Spirit that gave them forth ? You will say, Christ saith this, and the apostles say this ; but what canst thou say ? Art thou a child of Light and hast thou walked in the Light, and what thou speakest, is it inwardly from God ? " Such was the burden of his appeal. Margaret Fell, the Judge's wife, had risen in her pew, wondering at his words. She sat back weeping, cut to the heart, crying in spirit : " We are all thieves ! We are all thieves ! We have taken the Scriptures in words and know nothing of them in ourselves." Margaret Fell from that hour became George Fox's faithful friend, and her home was the nursery of the new fellowship of disciples, to which travelling preachers returned for help and counsel, and where Fox himself was always sure of a welcome and such brief rest as his strenuous mission would allow him.

Fox had made protest from the early days of his public service against treating the Christian ministry as a profession, which could be prepared for by a sufficient amount of study and be made a profitable career. But this did not make him careless for the human needs of those whose life call was to devotion to this high duty. Some of the early Quaker preachers had small properties of their own and needed no pecuniary help ; others returned at intervals to their farms or business and were able thus to support themselves ; while a number in less easy circumstances were set free for this work, which often involved constant travelling from place to place, by means of voluntary collections made regularly through the different groups of Quaker meetings. Fox himself was possessed of simple means which sufficed for his own modest wants and left him able to give some help to others. But no differences of rank or wealth marred the equal fellowship of this company of the " Publishers of Truth," as they were called by their friends.

During the Commonwealth Fox travelled through almost all parts of England and Wales as well as in Scotland, suffering repeated imprisonments—at Lancaster in 1652, then at Carlisle, and later for eight months in 1656 at Launceston, where he was confined with others for some time in a loathsome and verminous underground dungeon. On several occasions when in London he had noteworthy interviews with Cromwell, who was very friendly and allowed him to speak frankly to him, though latterly Fox's message was one of reproof for the persecutions permitted by the great Protector.

It was a time of hardship, but of tense enthusiasm and of wonderful fellowship amongst the groups of

Friends, who met together for the most part in farm kitchens or the halls of little country manor-houses and waited in prayerful silence on the unseen Heavenly Teacher. With a few the truth of the reality of the divine indwelling was misapprehended through ill-balanced minds or lack of humility ; and in the case of James Naylor this led to his allowing misguided followers to pay him Messianic honours, punished by Parliament with cruel scourgings and branding and the piercing of his tongue with a red-hot iron. Naylor bore his sufferings humbly, and showed deep penitence for the injury he had brought to the cause of Truth. Fox had reproved and separated from his friend before the sad event occurred, and there can be no doubt that it had a profound effect upon him. He never ceased to make the presence of the Light of Christ in the heart and all that it involved the central fact of his message, but he realized the danger into which James Naylor had fallen. "We are nothing ; Christ is all," was his way of putting in its proper relation the attitude of the individual believer to his Guide.

The Restoration was followed very shortly by the outbreak of fiercer persecution than had taken place under the Commonwealth ; over four thousand Quakers were thrown into prison in 1660. In spite of the protest made by Fox and other leaders that they did not believe in methods of violence or warfare and could not take up arms, they were suspected of plotting against the king. Fox himself was repeatedly imprisoned, facing his judges with unyielding courage, and with characteristic shrewd humour repeatedly getting the better of the argument in court before the inevitable sentence came. His health suffered severely, and many of the leading Quaker preachers died in prison. The storm of persecution sifted out the less stable elements, but only consolidated the Quaker fellowship. Meetings were kept up openly, in spite of the Conventicle Acts, sometimes even amid the ruins of meetinghouses that had been wrecked by the soldiery. Under the stress of trouble the religious organization of the Society, hitherto quite informal, was gradually brought into being. This had been no part of George Fox's ministry at the outset, for he had not aimed at the formation of a new denomination. His hope and thought, like those of the other pioneer Quaker preachers, were deeper and more universal. But as persecution deepened he felt a call to settle his Friends under "the true Gospel order." Fox, more than any other man, laboured to build up this organization, having to encounter fierce opposition in doing so, even from former colleagues. His constructive genius was shown in the grouping of meetings within reach of each other into "Monthly Meetings," which were to be the units for church business, these in turn forming through their representatives larger groups, known as "Quarterly Meetings," corresponding frequently to county divisions, and these again sending representatives to a "Yearly Meeting" for the whole country. From the first no votes were taken, decisions being reached through willingness to seek unity under the guidance of the Spirit. After some three years of hard imprisonment in Lancaster and at Scarborough, Fox travelled ceaselessly through the country to arrange for the setting up of these Monthly Meetings everywhere, and caused some difficulty among the less wide-minded by insisting on the necessity of similar meetings for women Friends, who had shared from the first, equally with men, in the work of the ministry in the Quaker fellowship. At first a large part of the work of the new meetings was in succouring the prisoners and their needy families, but they had also to deal with the religious needs of the congregation and the maintenance of a consistent way of life amongst individual members.

During this period, too, Fox urged the importance of education for the children of Friends, and succeeded in establishing two schools for boys and girls in the neighbourhood of London. He was particularly interested in the children learning on a wider basis than was customary in that day, wishing that girls as well as boys should be instructed " in whatsoever things were civil and useful in the creation."

In 1669 Fox travelled through Ireland, and on his return was united in marriage at Bristol with his friend, Margaret Fell, who had been a widow since 1658. She was the truest helpmeet to him, although the claims of his ministry in other parts allowed him but little home life with her at Swarth-more Hall. During the period of bitter persecution which broke out in 1670–1 Fox was laid aside by months of severe illness, which brought him to death's door ; but in August, 1671, though still weak and ill, he sailed to Barbados and visited, with other Quaker missionaries, Jamaica and the English colonies in America, passing through great physical hardships in his journeys on the mainland, and returning in the summer of 1673 to Bristol, where he was joined by his wife. His aged mother sent to ask him to visit her ere she died, but on his way he was arrested for attending a meeting and thrown into Worcester Gaol, and his mother failed to rally from the shock of the sad news. His release did not come till 1675, and most of the next two years were spent with his wife at Swarthmore Hall, when he was able to get the leisure to dictate his great *Journal* and to prepare a mass of letters and papers for use by subsequent writers. In 1677 he visited Holland and Germany, where groups of Quakers were already in existence, returning in 1678 to Swarth-more, which he left for work in the south of England in 1680. The remainder of his life, with the exception of a second visit to Holland in 1684, was principally spent in and around London, visit-ing the meetings of Friends and conducting a wide-reaching correspondence with invididuals and groups of Quakers in both continents. His body was worn out by hardships and sufferings, but to the end his spirit was active as ever. His wife came at intervals to visit him, but the call for each of them was to work in different parts, and they gave up the happiness of united home life to follow the call. While persecution lasted, he continued fearlessly to visit the Quaker meetings in London, on one occasion speaking in the street from a chair to the people when Gracechurch Street meeting-house was closed by force. He wrote or dictated letters and pamphlets, took a guiding part in the Yearly Meetings and other business gatherings, and at length had the joy of witnessing the passing of the Toleration Act in 1689.

In spite of increasing physical weakness, he was active to the end, which came in the first month of 1691 (1690 Old Style). After a meeting in Gracechurch Street, at which he had taken a remarkable part in preaching and prayer, he caught a chill on his way to his host's hard by, and passed peacefully away two days later. As he lay dying, he said to some Friends who visited him : " All is well : the Seed of God reigns over all, and over death itself."

William Penn, who had seen much of George Fox during his later years, has given us a fine portrait of the man as he knew him :

He was of an innocent life, no busy-body, nor self-seeker. . . . So meek, contented, modest, easy, steady, tender, it was a pleasure to be in his company. He exercised no authority but over evil, and that everywhere and in all ; but with love, compassion, and long-suffering. . . . I write my knowledge and not report. . . .

Having been with him for weeks and months together on divers occasions, and those of the nearest and most exercising nature, and that by night and by day, by sea and by land, in this and in foreign countries ; and I can say I never saw him out of his place, or not a match for every service or occasion. For in all things he acquitted himself like a man, yea, a strong man, a new and heavenly-minded man, a divine and naturalist, and all of God Almighty's making. . . . Civil, beyond all forms of breeding, in his behaviour. [After speaking of his ministry, Penn adds] : But above all he excelled in prayer. The inwardness and weight of his spirit, the reverence and solemnity of his address and behaviour, and the fewness and fullness of his words, have often struck even strangers with admiration, as they used to reach others with consolation. The most awful, living, reverent frame I ever felt or beheld, I must say, was his in prayer.

So one cannot wonder that the man who was so fearless and untiring in opposing the insincere and the self-seeking, who never quailed or bent before persecution and had to meet more than most men's lot of fierce opposition, anger, scorn, and hatred, awakened amongst those who responded to his appeal a deep and wonderful attachment, and for long after his death his Friends thought and wrote of him as " dear George Fox."

The Holborn Review, July, 1924.

GEORGE FOX

By John William Graham, M.A.

George Fox was born in July, 1624, and the Society of Friends, which he founded, is celebrating his Tercentenary this month. His birthplace was a village in Leicestershire, then called Drayton-in-the-Clay, now Fenny Drayton, but the strongest local interests of his life centre round the beautiful region which sends its streams down to Morecambe Bay. It is at Kendal, therefore, that the memorial celebrations are to be held.

Friends nowadays sometimes, realizing the smallness of their meetings and the limited appeal they manage to make to the religious instincts of the nation, say to one another : "Why cannot we shake the nation as George Fox did ? The views and principles we hold are essentially what his were, and make a similar appeal. Whereas we are told that every Quaker in George Fox's time would shake the country for ten miles round, we are of the quiet in the land, and most people hardly know where our meeting-house stands."

But the question is superficial. Something has gone from the nation since the time of the Protectorate and the Restoration. Particularly has the religious power of the country-side faded. I cannot conceive any movement now laying hold on the gentry and farmers, the shopkeepers and the labourers of North Lancashire and Westmorland, sending them to convert London and Bristol and the Colonies overseas to a faith which led them to abandon all their most sacred associations in church and sacrament, to take the Bible in a new way, and, in reliance on the Indwelling God, to go to prison, exile, or death with joy and newness of life.

The nation's interests and controversies at that time were in the main religious. When George Fox was born the emancipation from Rome was only as far away as the Corn Laws are from us. His mother, indeed, was " of the stock of the martyrs." Popery, prelacy, presbytery, and a host of minor systems and doctrines struggled for souls. Sermons were events as important as cricket matches are now, and Calvinism and Arminianism were debated as hotly as the Capital Levy. This prevailing religious tone had produced organizations strong for offence and defence, elaborate doctrine, anxiously precise practice, large endowments. The organizations had by George Fox's manhood come to be an end in themselves, as is the way of organizations ; though life might decay, endowments remained, sermons flowed, with frequent acrimony, and the struggle between Archbishop Laud and the Puritans had become an actual revolutionary war—

a war in which the constitutional issues were chiefly cared for because there was religious liberty or religious authority at stake behind them. This war, as wars do, further corrupted the spiritual temperament of the nation. It was thus to a people deeply committed to religion and yet under a yoke, a stiff framework to keep them to the orthodox furrow, that the Quaker message of freedom from human arrangements and external dogmas and professional clergy came, with its revival of the primitive Christian discovery of the divine in man, which mystics at all periods and in all faiths have rediscovered.

Moreover, the Early Friends spoke to people who had hardly any competing interests. The Puritans did not know about Shakespeare ; there were no novels, no magazines, no newspapers; there was no science and no British Empire. Foreign politics, concerning Holland and Spain, were religious issues. Serious-minded people gave their attention chiefly to the newly translated Bible. There were no football matches. The sporting world and the financial world hardly existed. There was little art outside churches, and hardly any foreign touring—indeed, very little home travel either.

Should a great religious genius arise, the fields were indeed white unto harvest. Much would depend on the man appearing. It has been our world calamity that in the war of 1914, and the period of disasters it has left, no great man—no man great enough for the task—has been in effective power for long in any large State. Hence these tears.

The greatness of George Fox grows upon us as we carefully study his career. He has not had an easy path to a great reputation outside Quakerism. He was poorly educated, no scholar, nor eloquent in style ; his opponents in the Anglican Church have been in power ever since, and have been the arbiters of reputations ; until this century there has been no good portrait of him in word or in picture. But there was enough in him, as I have written elsewhere, to make ten men great.

There were several departments of human greatness in which he achieved or suffered great things. There is some likeness, which I think is not fanciful, in his story, to the greatness and to the varied experiences of the Apostle Paul. We are reminded of George Fox when Paul tells of his own labours and sufferings amongst the false brethren and the Judaizers, of his task in building up the churches and suffering with all who suffered, his floggings, his shipwrecks, his public encounters with men in high places, his physical hunger and thirst and cold, his organizing gifts, mingled all the time with mystical experiences and visions and with lonely crucifixions for the sake of the world's sin. The Jews and Judaizers—who constituted the chronic worry of the life of Paul—were the same kind of people as the priests and professors whom George Fox confronted, with their external religion and

their spiritual pride. Paul concluded : " I have
finished my course ; I have kept the faith." George
Fox's last words were : " Now I am clear, I am
fully clear." With George Fox it was his letters
which were lumpy and ungrammatical, whilst his
bodily presence was powerful and awe-inspiring ;
but the Apostle of the Gentiles was capable of
writing weighty and powerful letters, though his
bodily presence was weak and his speech contempt-
ible. Nor could I quite imagine George Fox
ever being let down over a wall in a basket to escape
his enemies' hands. His way would rather have
been to walk up and down the market-place facing
them with his shining eyes. Those eyes were
one of his notable characteristics. The Cambridge
undergraduates, mobbing him as he rode through
their narrow streets, unhorsed his companion,
but could only call out round Fox : " He shines ;
he glisters ! "

George Fox wore his hair long in Cavalier rather
than Puritan fashion ; he used to walk miles on
the roads till his long imprisonment in Scarborough
Castle, in a room choked with smoke but open to
the wind and rain of that cliff-top overlooking the
North Sea. This suffering left him with his legs
swollen and his joints so stiff that he could hardly
mount his horse. This was at the age of forty-two.
He lived for a quarter of a century longer, but was
never a strong man again. He had the preacher's
gift of a great resonant voice, constantly used in
the open air. It rather frightened his judges in

the courts at Lancaster and elsewhere. William Penn says he was courteous beyond all forms of breeding. He was always " dear George " among his friends and followers. He held himself modestly when reverence and leadership came to him. He assumed no official position among the thousands who had gathered round him. For want of an official title he was generally described as " our worthy elder." William Penn says that he had been with him under all kinds of intimate experiences, but that he had never failed to find him ready for all occasions, whether it were taking to pieces an illegal warrant, or arguing with chaffy professors, or sitting in silence for hours on a haystack before an assembled multitude so as to starve them from words, or, again, preaching for three hours on Fir Bank Fell. He was able to speak with power face to face with Oliver Cromwell, and was equally willing to lie out at night among the wolves in an American swamp.

His courage is never known to have flinched. It is conspicuous on nearly every page of his *Journal*. When a new Conventicle Act was passed against Friends in 1670, he left his newly-wedded bride at Bristol to go to London, to Gracechurch Street, where he expected the persecution to begin, that he might be taken first. When the mob at Ulverston threw him to the ground, and left him for dead outside the town, he rose up again in the Lord's power, and when a blow from a great staff appeared to break his wrist and ruin his hand, he held it forth and it was cured, and he marched back to the town undismayed. "Stiff as a tree and as pure as a bell" was the verdict of the Governor of Scarborough Castle, who, in spite of his cruel treatment, became ultimately Fox's friend, and begged for a visit when his prisoner next came to Scarborough. Everywhere, indeed, his gaolers, however they began, became in the end his friends, and some joined the Society.

The central secret of a man's character, encumbered and sometimes baffled by the complications of adult life, may often be clearly seen in childhood. Pope tells us that he "lisped in numbers, for the numbers came." Tennyson and his brothers wrote poems on their slates in the nursery, and the child Ruskin preached to his cousin and nurse from a chair in the kitchen—"People, be dood." George Fox says :

When I came to eleven years of age I knew pureness and righteousness ; for while a child I was taught how to walk to be kept pure. The Lord taught me to be faithful in all things, and to act faithfully in two ways, viz. inwardly to God, and outwardly to man ; and to keep to Yea and Nay in all things. For the Lord showed me, that though the people of the world have mouths full of deceit, and changeable words, yet I was to keep to Yea and Nay in all things ; and that my words should be few and savoury, seasoned with grace ; and that I might not eat and drink to make myself wanton, but for health, using the creatures in their service, as servants in their places, to the glory of Him that created them ; they being in their covenant, and I being brought up into the covenant, as sanctified by the Word which was in the beginning, by which all things are upheld ; wherein is unity with the creation.

This paragraph shows the style of writing and preaching which William Penn in his testimony describes as " abrupt and broken, but full of substance." We have here the first uprush of the teaching of later years concerning plain and truthful speech, the care not to multiply words in religious services, and not to fear silence, moderation, and simplicity in regard to food and furniture, and, not least, a recognition of the universal harmony, a feeling of the sacramental significance of external happenings—particularly of human life—as one in nature with an Eternal Spirit.

It is not very surprising that his relatives thought that he should be made into a clergyman. He was, however, employed instead by a man who was a shoemaker and grazier, and sold wool and cattle, who was prosperous while George Fox worked for him, but not afterwards. In bargaining about the price of cattle, when he used the word " verily," that ended the matter, for people said : " If George says ' verily,' there is no altering him."

A proposal to him to drink to excess, made by two religious relatives, was the occasion which drove him, at the age of nineteen, from home. " The Lord said to me, Thou must forsake all, both young and old, and keep out of all, and be as a stranger unto all."

Four years of wandering over the Midland counties of England followed. He went as far as London, where, he says, " I looked upon the great

professors of the city, and I saw all was dark
and under the chain of darkness." This was the
year of Marston Moor. He came home after
about a year's absence, lest he should grieve his
parents. They prescribed the usual cure. "They
would have had me marry, but I told them I was
but a lad, and I must get wisdom." Others recom-
mended the army, "and I was grieved that they
proffered such things to me, being a tender youth."
He consulted religious authorities among priests
and professors—that is, among the Established and
the Separatist clergy—but all without success. He
was troubled about the ancient questions of pain
and evil, to which Calvinism only offered answers
that were worse than none. He reasoned with an
ancient priest about "the grounds of despair and
temptations," but was only bidden to take tobacco
and sing psalms. "Tobacco was a thing I did not
love, and psalms I was not in a state to sing."
Another experienced priest "I found only like an
empty, hollow cask." Another priest fell into a
great rage because, when walking with him on a
narrow path in his garden, the young man chanced
to set his foot on the side of a garden bed. "Thus
all our discourse was lost, and I went away in sorrow
worse than I was when I came." Another priest
thought that medical treatment was the best, and
tried to bleed the inquirer. "But they could not
get one drop of blood from me, either in arms or
head, my body being, as it were, dried up with
sorrows, grief, and troubles, which were so great

upon me that I could have wished I had never been born, or that I might have been born blind that I might never have seen wickedness or vanity, and deaf that I might never have heard vain and wicked words or the Lord's name blasphemed." This strange physical lack of circulation may be connected with his trances later. When the Christmas festivities were due, Fox "looked out poor widows from house to house and gave them some money" instead of joining in the revels.

From time to time he "had openings, and these openings agreed together," and he had "openings about the Scriptures," and "openings about one scripture agreed with openings about another." This was his unacademic way of saying that he gradually saw his way to a new system of coherent thought about God and man instead of the Puritan orthodoxy of the time. One of the openings, to which he refers frequently, "came to me as I was walking in a field on a First Day (that is Sunday) morning. The Lord opened to me that being bred at Oxford or Cambridge was not enough to fit and qualify a man to be a minister of Christ," and in that revelation we recognize the origin of the Quaker method of worship, with its rejection of a professional ministry. Another opening was "that God, who made the world, did not dwell in temples made with hands." These words of the Apostle Paul at Athens, though often quoted, he felt to be in contradiction to the established ideas. He saw that God's people were His temple, and that He dwelt in them. Here we note the beginning of the central doctrine of Quakerism, which finds in the spirit of man an organic outgrowth of the spirit of God.

In this restless seeking-time of doubt and anxiety George Fox experienced that dark night of the soul which all the great mystics record, times in which the soul, enclosed in the flesh, prone to folly and tossed by distractions, practises the spiritual athletics which are to lead, and do lead, to liberation and to light restored.

About the close of this preliminary period of strain, as he was walking by the church at Mansfield, the Lord said to him: "That which people trample upon must be thy food." He explains that what people trampled upon was the life of Christ : "They feed upon words, . . . but trample underfoot the blood of the Son of God ; which blood was my life, and lived in their airy notions, talking of him." By " airy notions " George Fox meant theological expositions, taking the place of real experience.

At this time there was one Brown, who upon his deathbed spoke of George Fox, and " what I should be made instrumental by the Lord to bring forth." On the day of Brown's funeral Fox fell into a trance, and appeared to be dead for fourteen days. He was much altered in countenance and person, as though his body had been " new moulded or changed." He had a sense and discerning given him by the Lord to the effect that when many people talked of God and Christ, " the serpent spoke in them ; but this was hard to be borne." But the vision was finally a vision of joy. " Yet the work of the Lord went on in some, and my sorrows and troubles began to wear off, and tears of joy dropped from me, so that I could have wept night and day with tears of joy to the Lord, in humility and brokenness of heart. I saw into that which was without end, and things which cannot be uttered, and of the greatness and infinitude of the love of God, which cannot be expressed by words. For I had been brought through the very ocean of darkness and death, and through and over the power of Satan, by the eternal, glorious power of Christ ; even through that darkness was I brought, which covered over all the world, and which chained down all and shut up all in death."

I will quote the great passage in which George Fox sums up the final triumph, in the strength of which he lived his fruitful life :

Now was I come up in Spirit through the flaming sword into the paradise of God. All things were new ; and all the creation gave another smell unto me than before, beyond what words can utter. I knew nothing but pureness, and innocency, and righteousness, being renewed into the image of God by Christ Jesus, to the state of Adam, which he was in before he fell. . . . Great things did the Lord lead me into, and wonderful depths were opened unto me, beyond what can by words be declared ; but as people come into subjection to the Spirit of God, and grow up in the image and power of the Almighty, they may receive the Word of Wisdom, that opens all things, and come to know the hidden unity in the Eternal Being.

GEORGE FOX

Between 1649 and 1675 George Fox suffered eight imprisonments, amounting altogether to about six years, in the noisome dens which were thought proper for penal purposes in the seventeenth century.

His first experience—for some weeks—was in " a nasty stinking " prison at Nottingham, in the year of the king's execution, for interrupting a preacher in church. To speak after the preacher had done was usual and allowed by Presbyterians. The next year he was sentenced to six months' imprisonment at Derby for blasphemy. Near the close of the time he was offered a commission in Cromwell's army, the command of a troop of soldiers who " said they would have none but him." He replied that he " lived in the virtue of that life and power that took away the occasion of all wars." " I told them I was come into the covenant of peace which was before wars and strifes were." This was the first Quaker Peace testimony, but it did not become a general tenet till 1659. His reward was a prophecy of the way the world would take such refusals. He was thrust " into the dungeon among the rogues and felons," without a bed to lie on, for six months more. The third imprisonment came in the year of the Protectorate, 1653, and it lasted seven weeks in Carlisle Castle, where what purports to be his miserable dark hole of a cell is still shown. The prisoners " were exceeding lousy," and the gaoler beat him with his great staff for going near the window. This cannot have been in the cell shown. Then the strange prisoner began to sing "in the Lord's power." This was countered by the gaoler bringing in a fiddle to drown his voice, " but my voice drowned them and struck them and confounded them ; that made them give over fiddling and go their ways."

In 1656 he spent eight months in Launceston and other gaols in Cornwall. In 1660 he was arrested at Swarthmoor and kept for four months in Lancaster Castle, and then a few weeks in London. It was on this occasion that fifteen men were assigned to guard him in the constable's house at Ulverstone. They sat close to the fire for fear their prisoner, with his strange powers, should go up the chimney. For had he not once been carried up to the clouds and been found afterwards with pockets full of gold and silver ? There marched thirty soldiers, horse and foot, with him across the sands of Morecambe Bay to Lancaster. His next imprisonment was at Leicester, for about a month. The next was the longest and the most cruel, at Lancaster and Scarborough, for two years and eight months. It was in the darkest days of the Anglican persecution, 1664–6, and his absence was acutely felt by Friends. His last, and eighth, imprisonment was in 1673–5, at Worcester, closing in London. During this time he dictated his *Journal* to Thomas Lower, his wife's son-in-law. Such is a brief summary of one of his avenues of service. The intervals of imprisonment were nearly all filled by travelling in the ministry.

The situation he found when he struggled on to his horse at Scarborough in 1666 was highly perilous for the infant Society. The early leaders were dead or in prison for the most part. He himself had been as a dead man for over two and a half years. The Society must be organized if it was to hold on. This would be done nowadays by circulars from headquarters in London or at Swarthmoor and a well-reported public meeting. But George Fox had not these facilities. For four years he travelled up and down the land, organizing Monthly and Quarterly Meetings, very much as they still exist. It was a great feat, for the Early Friends were not docile, but it is plain that Fox was a great organizer. Yet the process did lead to a small separation of people so dependent on the immediate promptings of the Spirit that even fixed times of meeting were abhorrent to them, and, oddly enough, so were women's meetings. This is known as the Wilkinson-Story Separation. Its strength was in Westmorland.

Fox's suffering under physical hardship was accompanied by a spiritual burden. It is not an easy gift to a man, this faculty of feeling the Divine Presence in him. The spiritual sensitiveness which apprehends that fact apprehends of necessity also the disharmony of men with the Universal Soul. "I came to know the hidden unity in the Eternal Being" is the last sentence in which he describes his illumination in the passage quoted above. "Unity with the creation" was a favourite phrase.

And the corresponding sense of storm and human shipwreck was also real and acute. No encasing husk of blindness or indifference protects souls like these from the impact of the darts of wrong and pain. Twice his spirit failed and dragged the body with it. The first time was at Reading, in 1659, the year of the collapse of militant Puritanism in mere egoism and confusion. Oliver was dead, and the leaders seemed to be "just plucking the Government down." It was the time of the prominence of Richard Cromwell, Monk, Lambert, Fairfax, and Ashley Cooper, and it brought the return of the Stuarts. The Kingdom of the Saints brought in by force was a lost hope. What, then, was the real hope? George Fox lay ill in great darkness for ten weeks.

While I was under that sore travail at Reading, by reason of grief and sorrow of mind, and the great exercise that was upon my spirit, my countenance was altered, and I looked poor and thin ; and there came a company of unclean spirits to me, and told me, " the plagues of God were upon me." I told them it was the same spirit spoke that in them, that said so of Christ, when he was stricken and smitten; they hid their face from him. But when I had travailed with the witness of God, which they had quenched, and had got through with it, and over all that hypocrisy which the outside professors were run into, and saw how that would be brought down, and turned under, and that life would rise over it, I came to have ease, and the light, power, and Spirit shone over all. And then having recovered, and got through my travails and sufferings, my body and face swelled, when I came abroad into the air ; and then the bad spirits said, " I was grown fat," and they envied at that also. So I saw, that no condition nor state

41

would please that spirit of theirs. But the Lord preserved me by his power and Spirit through and over all, and in his power I came to London again.

Immediately after, and, in my view, probably as the fruit of his travail on the failure of military Puritanism, George Fox issued a letter to Friends, bidding them

> Keep out of plots and bustling and the arm of flesh; for all these are amongst Adam's sons in the fall, where they are destroying men's lives like dogs, beasts and swine, goring, rending, and biting one another. . . . Whence arise wars and killing but from the lusts? . . . All that pretend to fight for Christ are deceived; for his Kingdom is not of this world, therefore his servants do not fight. . . . All that talk of fighting for Sion are in darkness; for Sion needs no such helpers.

This, the Quaker testimony against all war, had its birth, as a general tenet, in those ten weeks of striving at Reading.

The second illness was caused by the outbreak of persecution in 1670. "Near Rochester a great weight and oppression fell upon my spirit, so that I was hardly able to ride." In much weakness he reached the north shore of the Thames. At Stratford he lay in nervous collapse, having lost both hearing and sight. But he could discern the spirits of those who were with him, those who were honest-hearted and those who were not. When he was given up as dead, he ordered a coach to go twelve miles to Gerrard Roberts's, another sick man who needed encouragement. Thence to Amor Stoddart's—a dying man—who was told by George

Fox that " the immortal seed of life was his crown,"
though the speaker was hardly able to stand.   At
Widow Dry's at Enfield he lay all the winter,
" warring in spirit with the evil spirits of the world."

I was brought into the deep, and saw all the religions of the world,
and people that lived in them, and the priests that held them up,
who were as a company of men-eaters, eating up the people like
bread, and gnawing the flesh from off their bones.

If this appears harsh and one-sided, it may be
remembered in excuse that troops of horse were
breaking up meetings and meeting-houses, " and
some broke their swords, carbines, muskets, and
pikes with beating Friends ; and many were
wounded, so that their blood lay in the streets."

After eight months of this illness, and then a
successful effort with the king to get his wife out
of Lancaster Castle, the indomitable man set sail
on a mission to the West Indies and America, and
there he recovered.

The central formula of George Fox's gospel was
that by it the Lord had visited His people, after
long ages of apostasy, and that primitive Christianity
was now revived in the land.   His attack fell on
all the incrustations of symbolism, on all official
priestly functions and authority, on all routine in
ritual or prayers out of a book, on all paid preachers
with specialized training.

His freedom from tradition led him also to
attack those social habits which were based on
luxury and its companion, poverty.   William Penn

wrote that the trimmings of the vain world would clothe the naked one.   The appeal to the Indwelling God in all men led to a reverence for the lowest of mankind, and an utter loathing for murderous war, as a denial of the Spirit in man.

Theologically—in the treatment of such themes as the Incarnation, the Atonement, Forgiveness, Heaven and Hell—Fox was probably unconscious of making any change.   He accepted the Christian system he had been taught.   But his guiding principle left it open to Friends to modify these when no longer credible or no longer in harmony with the moral sense.   Forgiveness and Atonement from the beginning were regarded as inward transactions—the outward might be there too, but carried no emphasis.   Heaven and Hell were regarded as beginning on earth, which changes the idea radically from topography to experience.   The Incarnation found a place beside the doctrine of the Indwelling God.   Though they were unaware of it, the Early Friends were Modernists all the time, but Modernism was not their message nor their concern.   They had only two direct doctrinal controversies with the Puritans from whose midst they arose.   They attacked the doctrine of Election and Reprobation, with its corollary of human helplessness, and they asserted that sin was not essential to salvation nor to human life, and they denied imputed righteousness.   They believed in the possibility of Christian perfection, as in everything else which brought dignity and hope to poor humanity. George Fox himself never seems to have been conscious of a sense of personal sin. The Athanasian Trinity they took little interest in. They thought it " notional," i.e. speculative and outside experience. Fox's " gospel of silence " found a powerful convert in Carlyle. If convert is too definite a word, we may at least see in Carlyle's works clear signs of sympathy and conscious unity on this point between these prophets of the seventeenth and nineteenth centuries. What did they mean by it ? for they were both among the most vocal of men. It was superficialism in words that vexed their deeply original souls. Endless repetitions, prattling which is the mere expression of restlessness of mind, the dread of being thrown back on inward emptiness or discord, leading to talk for talk's sake—this was the verbosity they cried out against. God had no need of our words in His worship, only of the loyalty of our hearts. " Peace ; let us think." It is a good lesson, and our increasingly neurotic age needs it more than ever. With this call to silence there went in them both a mighty urge to reality, carrying with it a really fierce hatred of shams. It was natural that the Clothes Philosophy should bring in Fox's suit of leather, with a burst of admiration from the author of *Sartor Resartus*.

Has George Fox had a following worthy of his greatness and his originality ? He compares poorly as a founder with John Wesley, if you only count heads. But apart from the founder of Methodism,

45

is there any other individual leader who has left a larger mark on English religion ? Every other denomination is the confluence of many strains of influence. There is no one Baptist, Independent, Unitarian, Presbyterian, or Anglican founder in the same sense that George Fox alone originated Quakerism. His followers, too, although numbering only 20,000 in England, hold staff appointments in many armies of goodwill. The Society is neither dead nor dying. Friends hold with confidence to their ancient faith and with hope to their future service. The world will not cease to count upon them. Of how many spiritual conquerors in any age can that be said after three hundred years ?

The Hibbert Journal, July, 1924.

GEORGE FOX AND HIS RELIGIOUS
BACKGROUND

By Professor H. G. Wood, M.A.

There is a curious if somewhat idle fascination about the problem of origins in connection with the prophetic consciousness. Characteristic of prophecy is the sense of independence, the fresh, individual apprehension of truth. More often than not the prophet exaggerates his isolation. He feels that he alone is left, and is quite unaware of the seven thousand who have not bowed the knee to Baal. He is Browning's warrior, who cares not for doings right or left. He has his message to deliver, and he is not daunted if others gainsay it, nor does he sustain his confidence by amassing precedents. It seems almost impertinence to search for the sources of a prophet's message or even of a prophet's imagery in the records of his predecessors or contemporaries. Such inquiries are apt to deal with the circumstantial rather than the essential. They do not penetrate the prophet's secret. After all, the temple provides only the setting, not the source of Isaiah's vision of the Lord, high and lifted up.

If, however, there is some risk of losing sight of the prophet's true significance by tracing anticipations of or parallels to his message, yet some gains both to historical knowledge and spiritual understanding may be made in the process. We may thus come to appreciate the nature of revelation more fully. The idea of revelation as the miraculous communication from without of knowledge otherwise inaccessible to the prophetic mind is still widely current in pious circles. Along with it goes the conception of prophecy as the proclamation of facts which have no connection with the experience either of the prophet or his generations—statements of truth unintelligible alike to the inspired preacher and his audience. It is not necessary to deny the possibility and even the actuality of such an element in the prophetic experience both in the Old Testament and in Christian history. To take it as normative or as the highest type of prophecy is a fatal blunder in history and in religion. This would make the prophet at his best a kind of spiritual gramophone or possibly a spiritual parrot. This is neither the norm nor the ideal of prophecy. The inquiry after the possible sources of the content of the consciousness of any given prophet serves to bring out the links which bind him to his age. It also shows that God's revelations do not normally come without an apperceptive basis. It confirms a famous sentence of Locke's : "God, when He makes a prophet, does not unmake the man." For a true appreciation of a prophet and his message the study of parallels, previous and contemporary, is not unimportant.

RELIGIOUS BACKGROUND

In the case of George Fox, the founder of Quakerism, parallels to characteristic features of the thought and practice of his followers are not infrequent, and are full of interest. The Pilgrim Fathers, for example, under the leadership of John Robinson, made considerable provision for lay ministry, and approximated in the matter of Church discipline to the spiritual democracy which George Fox established later. Among the General Baptists who followed John Smyth high value was attached to the element of spontaneity in worship which was later to be one of the distinguishing characteristics of Friends. A closer parallel to more fundamental traditions is furnished in the teachings of Roger Brerely, a clergyman in Lancashire who died at Burnley in 1637. He was the founder of a group known as the Grindletonians, and he very powerfully influenced the Seekers in the north of England, from whom many of the early followers of George Fox came. He touches Fox most closely in his doctrine of faith, for he had the true Lutheran idea of faith. He preached faith as an inward trust in God which was to be carefully distinguished from mere notional orthodoxy. He also held that true faith should lead to victory over sin. A few lines from a rhymed defence written by Brerely may suffice to illustrate his position :

But this I saw, that there's a rest of faith,
Which sets Believers free from hell and death,
That out of us, our health and life is wrought,
That out of us, the same is to be sought.

49

That God's elect, even from their second birth
Unto their death, are strangers on the earth.
That precious liberty they hereby win,
How sweet a thing it is to master sin,
How this new Law doth set Believers free,
How Christ His yoke is perfect libertie;
How this can be, that men can part from ill,
When dangerlesse they may do what they will.

Here, as we shall see later, Brerely anticipates the essential polemic of Fox against the Puritans.[1]

The writings of Jacob Boehme, or Behmen, the inspired shoemaker of Goerlitz, also contained fundamental ideas that coincided with the message of George Fox. Behmen died in the year 1624—the year George Fox was born—and translations of some of his works began to be circulated in England twenty years later. Many expressions which Fox uses to describe his own experiences are the same as those used by Jacob Behmen. In particular the whole idea of the divine element in man as a seed is characteristic of the teaching of Behmen as it was of the teaching of George Fox. Perhaps this summary of the teaching of Behmen on this point, from the pen of Dr. Alexander Whyte, will suffice to bring out the coincidence between Behmenism and Quakerism:

Behmen appeals to all his readers, that if they will only go down deep enough into their own hearts—then, there, down there, deeper than indwelling sin, deeper than original sin, deep

[1] The best account of Brerely and of the relation of his teaching to the work of George Fox is given in a tract, *Zur Vorgeschichte des Quakertums*, T. Sippell.

down and seated in the very substance and centre of their souls—
they will come upon secret and unexpected seeds of Divine Life·
Seeds, blades, buddings, and new beginnings of the very life of
God the Son in their deepest souls.   Secret and small, Behmen
exclaims, as those seeds of Eden are, despise them not ; destroy
them not, for a blessing for thee is in them.   Water those secret
seeds, sun them, dig about them, and they will grow up in you
also.   The Divine Life is in you ; quench it not, for it is of God.
Nay, it is GOD Himself in you.   It depends upon yourself whether
or no that which is at this moment the smallest of all seeds is yet to
become in you the greatest and the most fruitful of all trees.[1]

So far as any formative influence on George Fox
himself is concerned, it is difficult to trace any
actual acquaintance on the part of Fox with the
writings of the men whose names we have just
passed in review. The *Journal* of George Fox
reveals hardly any traces of any other literary
influence besides that of the Scriptures.   It is not
indeed unlikely that in moving about among the
sectaries George Fox became familiar with characteristic expressions and thoughts that were derived
from Behmen ; but he probably had not read anything that Behmen wrote, and he was not conscious
of any debt to earlier religious teachers.   William
Charles Braithwaite rightly says in *The Beginnings
of Quakerism :* " The strong possibility of influences
of this kind having reached Fox does not prevent
William Penn's statement from being substantially
true that ' as to man, he was an original, being no
man's copy.' "   The interest taken in the writings
of Behmen in seventeenth-century England is more

[1] Alexander Whyte, *Jacob Behmen, an Appreciation*, pp. 81-2.

significant for the formation of the milieu of Fox than for the moulding of his mind. The spread of Behmenistic ideas helps to account not so much for the content of Fox's gospel as for the welcome it found.

Fox is frequently described as a mystic, and no doubt with a large measure of truth. Few men have been more conscious of the presence of God in human life, or more confident in the power of spiritual forces, and if trance and vision be regarded as characteristic of the mystic, then George Fox is worthy to be ranked with many other great names. But it is rather misleading to associate him with Behmen, or Swedenborg, or Plotinus. All three have a speculative, philosophical interest which is utterly lacking in Fox. Compared with such writers Fox will be found to move in a very narrow field, with a very limited range. Fox in his visions does not traverse heaven and hell ; he does not amass the material for a Divine Comedy, or even for the outline of a spiritual view of the universe. His visions for the most part have an immediate practical bearing on his own life and work, and this is indeed the most important contrast between Fox and Behmen. Behmen is concerned with some of the great speculative issues in the interpretation of Christianity to the world. Fox is concerned with the practical issue, which is no doubt a recurrent issue, but with which he had to deal in the particular circumstances of England in the time of the Civil War and the Commonwealth. He was facing the disillusionment and demoralization that accompanied and followed a great war, and his problem was the moral failure of traditional Christianity in general and of Puritanism in particular. In consequence, as we have already said, Fox is narrower in range than Behmen, but he is more intense in his preoccupation with the practical question, " What are Christians to do ? " He concentrates on very definite issues, and he is more aggressive, more missionary, than the great mystics with whom he is so frequently compared. Jacob Behmen sat down to write an answer to forty questions " which embodied some of the philosophical and theological problems which were agitating and dividing the learned men of that day." If such questions had been propounded to Fox he would probably have said that he had not come to dispute, but to remind men that they had sufficient light to live by.

In his concentration on the moral side of Christianity Fox showed himself to be a Puritan rather than a Mystic, and indeed his thought-forms are largely derived from Puritan teaching. His distinctive positions are his own reaction against elements of weakness in seventeenth-century Puritanism, and the strength of his ministry in no small degree lay here. He had, as William Penn says, " an extraordinary gift in opening the Scriptures." William Penn also says : " The mystery of the first and second Adam, of the fall and restoration, of the law and Gospel, of shadows and substance, of the servant's and Son's state, and the fulfilling of the Scriptures in Christ, and by Christ, the true Light, in all that are His through obedience of faith, were much of the substance and drift of his testimonies." [1] It will be clear that though Fox gave his own interpretation to the mystery of the first and second Adam, to the meaning of the Fall, and of the restoration of mankind in Christ, yet these great contrasts are derived from the Puritan teaching, of which they formed the framework. But it was the failure of Puritanism which underlay and conditioned his call to the ministry. As a small boy he had been perplexed by the low level on which professing Christians were content to live. He could see that professors did not possess the power of that which they professed, and it amazed him that Christian people could indulge themselves in wanton and needless excesses. Though he makes very little reference to the Civil War, there can be little doubt that this tremendous upheaval appeared to the young man, as he was then, as a great failure of Christianity. It was in July, 1643, when he was nineteen years old, that he left home and began wandering up and down the country in great distress of mind. Perhaps the most significant clue to the nature of his inner conflict is given in his well-known answer to Priest Stephens as to the meaning of the cry on the cross: " My God, My God, why hast Thou forsaken Me ? " " I told him that at that time the sins of

[1] *The Journal of George Fox*, Tercentenary Edition, p. xix.

all mankind were upon Him, and their iniquities and transgressions with which He was wounded, which He was to bear, and to be an offering for them as He was man, but died, not as He was God ; and so, in that He died for all men, and tasted death for every man, He was an offering for the sins of the whole world. *This I spake, being at that time in a measure sensible of Christ's sufferings and what He went through.*" [1] This certainly seems to suggest that Fox felt the Civil War to be a great moral failure of the nation and the Church. Men succumbed to temptations which they ought to have been able to resist, and his quest was the search for that power in Christianity which enables men to overcome temptation. His quest seemed to the average Puritan to be a vain and even presumptuous one. "We cannot expect," they urged, "to be free from sin while in the body and in this life." Consequently they suspected that Fox was in a morbid condition, and different ministers gave him practical advice which was doubtless well-intentioned, but which seemed to him to be trifling with the situation. One suggested that he should take tobacco and sing psalms ; another, thinking that it was a case for a doctor, advocated blood-letting—a panacea in the seventeenth century ; while his relations advised him to get married. They all assumed that he was in a condition of unhealthy melancholy, and that he ought to make some effort to cheer himself up ;

[1] *Journal,* Tercentenary Edition, p. 4. (Italics ours.)

but he knew that the problem with which he was wrestling went deeper than this. He felt that these Puritan teachers were well and at ease in that condition which was his pain, and he knew that a Christianity that was to save society must be morally more effective than Puritanism appeared to be in 1645.

It is not necessary to re-tell the story of the great discovery which enabled Fox to solve his problem. The essence of it was the realization that Christ was not just a figure in a dim, distant past, but a living guide whose presence may actually be known in the life of the individual believer. Or it may be put in another way in a phrase that is becoming popular at the present moment ; Fox discovered " the contemporary inspiration of the Holy Spirit." The Puritans believed in the work of the Holy Spirit in the Church, but they thought that in the inspiration of the Scriptures the work of the Holy Spirit had been of a character that was never to be repeated ; all subsequent inspiration was on a lower level. It was this doctrine that Fox felt himself obliged to challenge. It was the burden of his message that men must be guided by the same Spirit which gave forth the Scriptures. Indeed, only by the same Spirit could they really understand the Scriptures, and he held that the Puritan doctrine of an inspiration confined to the Scriptures, a doctrine which was intended to honour and exalt the Scriptures, did, as a matter of fact, close men's minds to the real significance of the

Scriptures. In describing the position he was led to take up at the beginning of his ministry, he speaks of this at some length :

I saw plainly that none could read Moses aright without Moses' spirit, by which Moses saw how man was in the image of God in Paradise, and how he fell, how death came over him, and how all men have been under his death. . . . I saw that none could read John's words aright, and with a true understanding of them, but in and with the same divine spirit by which John spake them ; and by his burning, shining light, which is sent from God. Thus I saw it was an easy matter to say death reigned from Adam to Moses ; and that the law and the prophets were until John ; and that the least in the kingdom is greater than John ; but none could know how death reigned from Adam to Moses, etc., but by the same Holy Spirit that Moses, the prophets, and John were in. They could not know the spiritual meaning of Moses', the prophets', and John's words, nor see their path and travels, much less see through them and to the end of them into the kingdom, unless they had the spirit and light of Jesus ; nor could they know the words of Christ, and of his apostles, without his spirit. But as man comes through by the spirit and power of God, to Christ who fulfils the types, figures, shadows, promises and prophecies that were of him, and is led by the Holy Ghost into the truth and substance of the Scriptures, sitting down in him who is the Author and end of them ; then are they read and understood with profit and great delight.[1]

He comes back again and again to this essential point. It led him to question publicly the customary teaching of Puritan ministers. At the very outset of his career as an apostle he went into a church at Nottingham, where the following incident took place :

[1] *Journal,* Tercentenary Edition, p. 19.

57

When I came there all the people looked like fallow ground, and the priest like a great lump of earth, stood in his pulpit above. He took for his text these words of Peter : " We have also a more 'sure Word of prophecy, whereunto ye do well that ye take heed, as unto a light that shineth in a dark place, until the day dawn, and the day-star arise in your hearts." And he told the people that this was the Scriptures, by which they were to try all doctrines, religions and opinions. Now the Lord's power was so mighty upon me, and so strong in me, that I could not hold, but was made to cry out and say, " Oh, no, it is not the Scriptures." But I told them what it was, namely, the Holy Spirit, by which the holy men of God gave forth the Scriptures, whereby opinions, religions, and judgments were to be tried ; for it led into all Truth, and so gave the knowledge of all Truth. The Jews had the Scriptures, and yet resisted the Holy Ghost and rejected the Christ, the bright morning-star. They persecuted Christ and His apostles, and took upon them to try their doctrines by the Scriptures, but erred in judgment and did not try them aright because they tried without the Holy Ghost.[1]

This exaltation of the present guidance of the Holy Spirit above the letter of the Scriptures was most offensive to the Puritan mind. In open court in Lancaster, in 1652, the magistrate gave him the opportunity of speaking to the people, and Fox writes as follows :

I was moved of the Lord to speak ; and as soon as I began, Priest Marshall, the orator for the rest of the priests, went away. That which I was moved to declare was this : that the Holy Scriptures were given forth by the Spirit of God, and all people must first come to the Spirit of God in themselves, by which they might know God and Christ, of whom the prophets and the apostles learnt ; and by the same Spirit know the Holy Scriptures ; for

[1] *Journal,* Tercentenary Edition, p. 24.

as the Spirit of God was in them that gave forth the Scriptures, so the same Spirit of God must be in all them that come to understand the Scriptures; by which Spirit they might have fellowship with the Son, and with the Father, and with the Scriptures, and with one another; and without this Spirit they can know neither God nor Christ, nor the Scriptures, nor have the right fellowship one with another.[1]

This characteristic utterance of Fox produced the usual antagonism in the minds of Puritan ministers. He continues in his *Journal:* " I had no sooner spoken these words than about half a dozen priests who stood behind me burst out into a passion." One of them proceeded to argue that the Spirit and the letter were inseparable, urging, no doubt, that you could only have the guidance of the Spirit by honouring the letter of the Scriptures. Fox replied : " Then everyone that hath the letter hath the Spirit ; and they might buy the Spirit with the letter of the Scriptures." And the magistrates felt the truth of this, and told the ministers that according to their position they might carry the Spirit in their pockets as they did the Scriptures. Fox was concerned to show that reverence for the Scriptures did not necessarily mean submission to the Spirit of God. This position of Fox's naturally seemed revolutionary to the Puritans, and it is clear that Fox, in claiming that he had a word from the Lord as sure as any of the apostles ever did, and that he received the truth that was given to him in the light of the Lord Jesus Christ and

[1] *Journal,* Tercentenary Edition, p. 78.

by His immediate Spirit and power as did the holy men of God, by whom the holy Scriptures were written, was making a very revolutionary claim. He was, as a matter of fact, putting the fundamental Christian objection to the bibliolatry that is now known as " Fundamentalism." Fox was in no sense a higher critic, though he recognized the progressive character of revelation in the Bible. He did not object to the Puritan view of the Scriptures because of intellectual difficulties. His quarrel with the Puritan doctrine of inspiration was that it deprived the average Christian of his birthright. He thought, not that the Puritans took too high a view of the inspiration of the Scriptures, but that they took too low a view of the possibilities of inspiration in ordinary Christian living. In consequence, they honoured the Scriptures while dishonouring the Holy Spirit.

His second main criticism of the Puritan position was closely bound up with his protest against their view of the Scriptures. The Puritans generally believed that the conflict with sin must continue in the heart of the believer so long as he was in the body. Fox believed that the Christian was not condemned to an unending conflict with the same recurrent temptations, but that he might enter into an experience of victory here and now. He believed in the reality of sanctification. In this his attitude differs somewhat from that of Behmen, who is nearer to the Puritan position. Behmen could write as follows :

" The truth of God did burn in my bones till I took pen and ink and began to set down what I had seen. All this time do not mistake me for a saint or an angel. My heart also is full of all evil. In malice, and in hatred, and in lack of brotherly love, after all I have seen and experienced, I am like all other men. I am surely the fullest of all men of all manner of infirmity and malignity." Behmen protests in every book of his that what he has written he has received immediately from God. " Let it never be imagined that I am any greater or any better than other men. When the Spirit of God is taken away from me I cannot even read so as to understand what I have myself written. I have every day to wrestle with the devil and with my own heart, no man in all the world more." [1]

Fox would proclaim as emphatically as Behmen his utter dependence upon Christ ; he would say, as Behmen says: " Thou must not for one moment think of me as having already by my own power or holiness climbed up into heaven or descended into the abyss " ; but he does not write with the consciousness of sin that you find expressed in the words we have just quoted from Behmen. He writes much more confidently of the experience of sanctification. The examination of Fox at Derby in 1650 is very significant. He is brought before the magistrates soon after midday.

They asked me why we came hither. I said, " God moved us so to do " ; and I told them, " God dwells not in temples made with hands." I told them also all their preaching, baptism and sacrifices would never sanctify them ; and bid them look unto Christ in them and not unto men ; for it is Christ that sanctifies.

Then they ran into many words ; but I told them that they were
not to dispute of God and Christ, but to obey Him.   The power
of God thundered amongst them, and they did fly like chaff before
it.   They put me in and out of the room often, hurrying me back-
ward and forward ; for they were from the first hour till the ninth
at night in examining me.   Sometimes they would tell me in a
deriding manner that I was taken up in raptures.   At last they asked
me whether I was sanctified.   I answered, " Sanctified ! yes " ; for
I was in the paradise of God.   Then they asked me if I had no
sin.   I answered, " Sin !   Christ, my Saviour, has taken away
my sin, and in Him there is no sin."   They asked how we knew
that Christ would abide in us.   I said, " By His Spirit that He has
given us."   They temptingly asked if any of us were Christ.   I
answered, " Nay, we are nothing ; Christ is all."   They said, " If
a man steal, is it no sin ? "   I answered, " All unrighteousness is
sin." [1]

The magistrates committed him to prison, and
Fox thus describes his experiences during his imprisonment :

While I was in prison many people came from far and near to
see a man that had no sin ; and divers of the professors came to
discourse with me ; and I had a sense before they spake that they
came to plead for sin and imperfection.   I asked them whether
they were believers and had faith, and they said " Yes."   I asked
them, " In whom ? " and they said, " In Christ."   I replied, " If
ye are true believers in Christ you are passed from death to life ;
and if passed from death, then from sin that bringeth death.   And
if your faith be true, it will give you victory over sin and the Devil,
purify your hearts and consciences (for the true faith is held in a
pure conscience), and it will bring you to please God and give you
access to Him again."   But they could not endure to hear of purity
and of victory over sin and the Devil, for they said they could not

[1] *Journal*, Tercentenary Edition, p. 30.

believe that any could be free from sin on this side of the grave. I bid them give over babbling about the Scriptures, which were holy men's words, whilst they pleaded for unholiness.[1]

It may reasonably be argued that the confidence of Fox in the completeness of his sanctification was strengthened by his acceptance of the Puritan belief that the inspiration of the Scriptures carried with it infallibility and inerrancy. Believing as he did that inspiration was as much a reality in the seventeenth century as in the first, he could not but believe that the same freedom from error might be conferred on Christians in the seventeenth century as he supposed the writers of the New Testament enjoyed. But sanctification for him was an actual experience, not a deduction from a doctrine about the nature of inspiration. He knew that in the New Testament inspiration meant spiritual insight and moral strength, and he found the same wisdom and power through the same Spirit in his own life. In consequence he was led to challenge all sorts of social customs and moral conventions which seemed tolerable to the ordinary Christian conscience in the seventeenth century. Some of these primitive Quaker testimonies, such as the refusal to use the ordinary names of the months and days of the week, seem to us lacking in a sense of proportion ; others reveal a moral perception greatly in advance of the age in which Fox lived. It is, for example, very significant that Fox realized and emphatically condemned the

[1] *Journal*, Tercentenary Edition, p. 32.

iniquity of the free use of capital punishment for minor crimes two hundred years before the iniquity was actually abolished in the British administration of justice. He also perceived very clearly the sin of intolerance—the sin of that moral indignation which so many of his contemporaries regarded as part of the service of God. Again and again he comes back to the simple point that men who cannot keep their tempers are not under the guidance of the Spirit. The following conversation with a Welsh magistrate is typical of Fox's standpoint :

> So then he began to ask me whether I owned election and reprobation. " Yes," said I, " and thou art in the reprobation." At that he was up in a rage and said he would send me to prison till I proved it ; but I told him I would prove that quickly if he would confess the Truth. Then I asked him whether wrath, fury and rage and persecution were not marks of reprobation ; for he that was born of the flesh persecuted him that was born of the Spirit ; but Christ and His disciples never persecuted nor imprisoned any. Then he fairly confessed that he had too much wrath, haste and passion in him. I told him Esau was up in him, the first birth, not Jacob, the second birth. The Lord's power so reached and came over him that he confessed to Truth.[1]

The Puritan did not normally regard the persecuting spirit as evidence of reprobation. As is apparent from this passage, Fox cared very little about election and reprobation as theological problems. All that he was interested in was the moral equivalent of these theological terms.

[1] *Journal,* Tercentenary Edition, p. 146.

RELIGIOUS BACKGROUND

To his contemporaries Fox appeared to be a simple man—and in truth he was a simple man. His message was confined to one or two leading ideas which he put with great plainness and homeliness, and which he did not hesitate to repeat in the same language over and over again. But his very simplicity was disconcerting, for he brought men back again and again to the moral reality at once of their creed and their life. He called men to a more sincere recognition of their sins, and inspired them with the hope of a more complete salvation. " I directed them to the Divine Light of Christ and His Spirit in their hearts which would discover to them all the evil thoughts, words and actions they had thought, spoken and acted, by which Light they might see their sin and also their Saviour Christ, Who is sent to save them from their sins." He spoke little of forgiveness or justification or of escape from the consequences of sin, and directed men's attention to the possibility of being liberated from sin itself, of rising to higher things. He thus made a unique contribution to the re-fashioning of social and religious life in England during the degradation of the Restoration period. The challenge which he gave to seventeenth-century England is not irrelevant to the circumstances of to-day, and the hope which he held out to his contemporaries will not prove illusory to a later generation.

The Holborn Review, July, 1924.

THE PSYCHOLOGY OF GEORGE FOX

By RUFUS M. JONES, LL.D.,
Professor of Philosophy in Haverford College.

THE three-hundredth anniversary of the birth of George Fox will send many persons back to read the rugged story of his life, and it will waken or refresh a general interest in that picturesque personality of the English Commonwealth. If Fox himself saw this title he would have no idea what it was about or what it meant. It was not the custom in his day to " psychologize " nor to assume that a man's personality and mission could be " explained " by an analysis of his dreams, his reveries and his dominant sentiments ! And yet one of the greatest English psychologists that ever lived, Thomas Hobbes, walked the same streets with him, and a greater than Hobbes, John Locke, the father of English psychology, spanned almost exactly the same period of years that Fox himself did.

But I have no illusions about the magic power of psychology. It has discovered no miraculous method of diagnosis. The solemn secrets of the soul are still kept. The ultimate mysteries of personality have not been invaded. As of old the winds of God, the tremulous movings of the Spirit, are uncharted. We do not know how self-consciousness emerges, how the distinction of right and wrong is born, how in a world of determined movements the will of man is autonomous and free, how the personal self becomes an ideal-forming being, how without " senses " for it the soul nevertheless attains the power of *vision* and rises, or may rise, to a certainty of communion with a Great Companion. Psychology is young ; it will do well in these days of minority to remain humble and somewhat shy.

But in spite of this honest confession it nevertheless remains true that we have discovered many significant clues that help us to interpret human character. We know more than Hobbes or Locke did about certain psychical traits and dispositions. It is not just an accident that it was Fox, and not Bunyan or De Foe, who was the mystic and who experienced the illumination of an inward light. We do not know, perhaps, why a certain unstable condition of brain and nerves—a slight tendency, it may be, toward disintegration or dissociation—should make a person more likely to become a genius or a mystic, but at least we do know that this is a fact. The tighter, compacter formation is " safer." Where the neurons of the brain are firmly bound together and the interlocking bridges —the synopses, as they are called—are solidly built up, there is not likely to be a new or dangerous or explosive type of character. Such an one has

67

given hostages to fortune that he will keep the peace and walk the safe, level paths of life. It is the person strung like a Stradivarius violin—delicate, mysterious, unique, incalculable—it is that kind of person who writes "The Ancient Mariner" or who leads a new religious movement. When we talk about the psychology of George Fox we do not pretend to go behind appearances and to explain how the Spirit works, how religion is born, how I am I and he is he, but only to trace the outward signs and visible intimations which indicate the kind of person we are dealing with. I propose to use as little as possible of the technical jargon of psychology.

George Fox was plainly enough a person with well-marked psychical traits and disposition, one in whom the normal and the abnormal kept house together. These two terms, "normal" and "abnormal," are not thoroughly fixed and sharply defined. For some who use them, "normal" means being as people usually are, doing as they usually do, conforming to the norm and standard; while to be "abnormal" means to deviate from what is expected, to be peculiar and unusual. On the other hand, some use the words in a more exact sense. "Normal" now means rational and constructive; "abnormal" means irrational and "defeative"—it denotes the possession of attitudes and acts which tend to hamper sane and intelligent ends of life. George Fox's early life reveals, as we shall see, abnormal traits in both these senses.

In the formative period of childhood, when the lines of personality are beginning to take shape, very important organizing tendencies come to light. At first all acts are instinctive, the springs and tendencies of response having been organized in the neural structure before the child was born, but gradually, with the dawning of intelligence, the instincts themselves and the emotions that are attached to them, become organized into little systems for the accomplishment of certain desirable ends. Little by little the ends or aims become conscious purposes, loaded with interest and meaning. These purposes become ideals to be striven for, and around these purposes or ideals many instincts, impulses, emotions and intentions are organized into unified systems of life. These systems are the foundations of all our loyalties and of all our purposeful activities. These organized systems are nowadays called *sentiments*, and they come to be our greatest driving forces. But sometimes these systems are organized around a " submerged " purpose, a purpose of which the individual himself is unconscious. This is usually due to the suppression of some powerful instinctive emotion, frequently to the suppression of some fear. The instinctive springs and forces are organized as completely as in the case of a normal sentiment, only the end and purpose of it is below the threshold of consciousness, unknown or unrecognized by the person himself. Such a system of emotional springs is in modern terminology called a " complex," and if it is a powerful one and goes on working submerged and suppressed it may, and often does, play havoc with the personality—it may produce hysteria, with all its complicated forms of automatisms, anæsthesia, auto-suggestion, dissociation, trance, or even divided personality.

It will perhaps seem ruthless and cold-blooded to deal with this great spiritual leader as though he were a common " pathological subject." But the lover of truth will not care to wear blinders as he reads the biography of saints, and if he is familiar with the impressive facts of evolving progress from the low and mean and humble on up to the crown and pinnacle of things, he will rejoice to see here an almost marred and broken human vessel reorganized, unified and integrated by his discovery and his faith, purified by his sufferings, fused and kindled by the love of Christ, and he will quietly say, as I do : " The important question is not what we came from, but rather where we *arrive and whither we are bound !* "

We have too little definite information in Fox's vivid and admirably expressed autobiographical account of his youth given in the *Journal* to tell precisely and exactly " how it was with him," to use his own phrase. He was obviously a " peculiar " boy, but there is no proof in sight to show that he was in a pathological condition. " In my very young years," he says, " I had a gravity and stayedness of mind and spirit not usual in children," but certainly more usual, we may add, in those days of Puritan ideals than in 1924. We should think something was the matter if we had such a child or saw such a child now ! He proceeds to say : " When I came to eleven years of age, I knew pureness and righteousness, for while a child I was taught (divinely taught, I suppose he means) how to walk to be kept pure." " The Lord showed me that I was to keep to Yea and Nay in all things."

There is no way of discovering just how much he means by phrases such as " the Lord showed me," " the Lord taught me," " the Lord said to me." They may be used freely and loosely for the fact that he had an " impression " or that it was " borne in upon his mind," or, on the other hand, he may mean, as he often does *seem* to mean, that he actually heard voices—what are known as " auditions." I am inclined to think that the first and simpler explanation is the right one at this early stage. And I see no reason for concluding that Fox had any marked pathological symptoms before he was nineteen, though he was evidently a boy apart from others—lonely, introspective and acutely con-scientious—but there is no evidence that he was morbidly so. He was the kind of boy that would be deeply impressed and probably oppressed by the sermons of the Rev. Nathaniel Stephens, who came to be curate in the Fenny Drayton church in 1638, becoming rector of it in 1659. Fox would thus be fourteen before he heard this particularly intense brand of Calvinism, while his religious seriousness long antedates that period. It can, however, be said emphatically that the episode at the fair which occurred when he was nineteen would not have produced such a mental upheaval if all had been well with him up to that day. In any case, this episode marks a distinct epoch in his life. He had gone to a nearby town on business at a fair with a cousin and another companion who was a " professor," i.e. a church member. They went to a public-house and drank a jug of beer together. This seemed all right, as it was taken solely to quench thirst. But the other two men began to " drink healths," calling for more beer and saying that he who would not drink should pay the entire reckoning. Fox laid a small piece of money on the table and left them. " I returned home," he says, " but did not go to bed that night, nor could I sleep, but sometimes walked up and down and sometimes prayed and cried to the Lord, *Who said unto me:* ' Thou seest how young people go together into vanity and old people into the earth ; thou must forsake all, both young and old, and keep out of all and be as a stranger unto all.' " [1]

Then came " a command of the Lord " to " leave home and relations "—i.e. family—and to " break off all fellowship with old and young." He now became an exile and a wanderer, travelling through towns and hamlets, declining to talk even with kindly disposed " professors," being " sensible that they did not possess what they professed." He went through a strong " temptation to despair,"

[1] *Journal,* Eighth Edition, vol. i. p. 3.

and had " mighty troubles." He kept solitary and apart from men, and wondered why these experiences should have come to him, and he said to himself, " Was I ever so before ? " Then he wondered whether he did right to " forsake " his " relations," and he searched his soul to see whether he had " wronged any." Powerful temptations beset him, and he got the impression that Satan was laying " snares and baits " to draw him to " commit some sin." This condition and state of affairs lasted three or four years, a good deal of which time he was on the verge of despair and in great trouble, but obviously not conscious of sin, as he is careful to say that he was only *tempted* to sin without actually committing the sin. Then he had a period of " looking to priests for comfort " —there was no comfort in them. Next he tried the Baptists in London, where his uncle Pickering lived. He found the Baptists " tender "—i.e. truly pious—but he was not free to impart his mind to them nor to join them, " for," he says, in a significant and revealing phrase, " *I saw all, young and old, where they were.*" [1]

The ground and basis of his mental trouble was pretty clearly the fixed idea that there existed in England—and so far as he knew, in the world— no genuine, vital, spiritual Christianity, no Christianity of primitive, apostolic, *overcoming and saving* power. Not only was there nothing of that sort to be found, but furthermore he knew not how to

[1] *Journal,* Eighth Edition, vol. i. p. 4.

inaugurate that type of religion himself. The old was hollow, formal and dead, and the new was not born yet. That, I feel sure, is the source of his sorrows and his troubles. It has always been somewhat of a mystery why George Fox should have had such a marked crisis and should have passed through such a prolonged period of agony when he shows no personal conviction of sin in his own case. The secret, I am convinced, lies just where I have found it, namely, in his momentous discovery that existing religion was bankrupt, and that no one any longer possessed apostolic power.

After many travels that brought no results Fox returned home, since he was uneasy in mind over his separation from his family, and he spent about a year at this time in Drayton. He had talks with Priest Stephens, who used Fox's religious views to adorn his sermons. He tried other priests in nearby towns, but they were " miserable comforters," " empty, hollow casks," all of them unable to " speak to his condition." At this period, when Fox was about twenty-three, appeared a striking symptom of his mental state. A priest in high account wanted to have him bled, in the hope, after the practice of that period, that it would improve his physical condition, but Fox adds : " They could not get one drop of blood from me, either in arms or head, though they endeavoured to do so, my body being, as it were, dried up with sorrows, grief and troubles which were so great upon me that I could have wished that I had never been born, *or that I had been born blind, that I might never have seen wickedness or vanity; and deaf, that I might never have heard vain and wicked words."* [1] The first point to note in the narrative which I have italicized is the state of mind which still possesses him regarding the hopeless religious condition of the world, " wickedness and vanity " in the lives of " professors." He would have preferred to be blind or deaf so that he might not have perceived it. On at least one occasion he was actually " struck blind " and " could not see " for a time.[2] Blindness from auto-suggestion is a well-known trait of persons in the condition in which Fox found himself during these years of agony.

His own explanation of the failure to get blood from him is quite inadequate—there was no doubt a normal quantity of blood in him. The incident is a plain indication, a major symptom, of hysteria. Another incident which came somewhat later, but probably the same year, reveals still profounder symptoms. There was a man named Brown who on his deathbed prophesied much about Fox, and had a " sight " of what he was later to accomplish. " When this man was buried," the *Journal* says, " a great work of the Lord fell upon me, to the admiration (i.e. wonder) of many, who thought I had been dead (he evidently lay in trance condition) ; and many came to see me for about fourteen days. I was very much altered in countenance and person, as if my body had been new moulded or changed.

[1] *Journal,* Eighth Edition, vol. i. p. 6.   [2] Ibid., p. 27.

While I was in that condition I had a sense and discerning," [1] i.e. he was telepathic and could read or at least get a glimpse of other minds in the room with him.

It is not difficult to parallel these experiences from the autobiographies of the great mystics and from the lives of other religious leaders, but none who know about such conditions would think of calling them normal occurrences. Fox alternated from experiences in the deeps to experiences in the heights. He says : " I fasted much and walked abroad in solitary places many days, and often took my Bible and went and sat in hollow trees and lonesome places till night came on, and frequently in the night walked mournfully about by myself." " I had some intermissions and was brought into such a heavenly joy, that I thought I had been in Abraham's bosom." [2]

During this long time of search and inward struggle the young man had many " openings." He means by the apt phrase that some truth was revealed as in a flash to his soul, so that he vividly saw that the truth was true. In a number of cases he uses the words, " I saw," so emphatically that he appears to mean that he visualized the experience. A passage like this illustrates it : " They were discoursing of the blood of Christ, and as they were discoursing of it, *I saw*, through the opening of the Invisible Spirit, the blood of Christ. And I cried out among them and said, ' Do ye not see the blood

[1] *Journal*, Eighth Edition, vol. i. p. 20.   [2] Ibid., p. 10.

76

of Christ ?   See it in your hearts to sprinkle your hearts and consciences from dead works, to serve the living God.' " [1]   The most wonderful of all his " openings " is a *vivid sight* of the reality of which he speaks : " I *saw* that there was an ocean of darkness and death ; but an infinite ocean of light and love that flowed over the ocean of darkness. In that also I saw the love of God." [2]   Another important visualizing passage dated in 1652 describes his first discovery of groups of Seekers in the northern counties.   The experience anticipates the actual finding of the groups.   " From the top of this hill (Pendle Hill) the Lord let me *see* in what places He had a great people to be gathered." A little later, in an inn, after he had descended the hill, he had an extension of his vision : " The Lord opened unto me, and let me *see* a great people in white raiment by a river side coming to the Lord. And the place that I saw them in was about Wensleydale and Sedbergh." [3]   Some of his " openings " appear to have surged up into his consciousness when he was not thinking at all of the subject.   The " opening " seemed to be " given " to him from the unseen beyond.   Here is a good example of what I mean : " The Lord opened to me that being bred at Oxford or Cambridge was not enough to fit and qualify men to be ministers of Christ."   At another time the Lord " opened " to him that only those who were born of God and had passed

[1] *Journal,* Eighth Edition, vol. i. p. 24.   [2] Ibid., p. 19.
[3] Ibid., pp. 109–10.

from death to life were *true believers*. Again :
" It was opened unto me by the Eternal Light and
Power, and I saw clearly therein ' that all was
done and to be done, in and by Christ.' " Once
more he says : " The Lord opened to me by His
Invisible Power that every man was enlightened
by the Divine Light of Christ." All these " openings " had to do with truths that had already been
proclaimed by the spiritual reformers or by some
of the small sects in England that had been inspired
by these leaders. The truths were not *new*, but
they came with fresh and living force into the
consciousness of Fox, and they possessed extraordinary meaning and driving power for him.
The greatest of all these first-hand experiences and
the most transforming of them all is the one that
marked the turning-point in his discovery of an
apostolic Christianity : " When all my hopes in
all men were gone so that I had nothing outwardly
to help me, nor could I tell what to do ; then, oh
then, I·heard a voice which said : ' There is One
even Christ Jesus that can speak to thy condition ' ;
and when I heard it, my heart did leap for joy,"
and now, he adds, " I knew experimentally." " I
knew God by revelation as he who hath the key
did open." [1]

This experience of inward certainty, together
with the no less impressive one when he " came up
in Spirit through the flaming sword into the paradise
of God," so that the whole creation gave a new

[1] *Journal*, Eighth Edition, vol. i. pp. 11–12.

smell, and he found himself in the condition Adam was in before he fell,[1] put him on his feet with his face toward the light. There were other flashes of the certainty of the love of God, and he came more and more into an abiding consciousness that he possessed the light and life and love and salvation of God in his own soul.

These experiences constituted for Fox *his spiritual stock*. The collapse and agony, which upset his equilibrium, had been due to the discovery that Christianity was dull, formal, hollow and dead—a sham and a mockery. This conclusion was hasty, not founded upon very wide experience, but, like so many other things in his life, he suddenly *saw it*, and his entire house of faith and hope collapsed. The prevailing religion of dogma, of theory, of words and notions, with little *life and power* to back it, seemed to him no better than no religion at all. He broke with the Church and went out into a world in which he could find no organization apparent that was carrying on and continuing the religion of Christ's gospel, a religion grounded in life and experience and marked by miraculous transforming power. Now at length he had discovered this in himself. He knew that he had passed from death to life, that he had found the living Christ, that his religion did not rest on a book or a creed, but upon an experience of God and of the power of His salvation. He had something to say and to exhibit, and he believed himself

[1] *Journal*, Eighth Edition, vol. i. p. 28.

sent forth with this foundation basis for a revival
of apostolic faith and Christianity.

There comes, almost at once, a reorganization of
his shattered physical system. He was not made
over in a minute, of course, but the integration
becomes apparent as soon as the constructive discovery was made and he had found his marching
orders. He was naturally a " motor " type of man ;
he was not made for contemplation and beatific
vision, but for action and deeds. The *Journal* is a
book of travel, of events, of activity. He did not
find himself until he found his constructive idea—
then he can " shake the world for ten miles around,"
and even into wider circuits. It must be said,
however, that his first four years of ministry—
1648 to 1652—were not very successful, and they
brought upon him much brutal treatment. He did
not yet find many prepared groups, and he gathered
only scattered followers. He was under constant
strain and had terrible prison experiences, so that
it is not strange that there were some recurrent
symptoms of his old trouble—the Lichfield episode,
for instance. But in 1652 he came upon the
great groups of Seekers in Yorkshire and Westmorland, and they recognized in him at once the
apostolic leader for whom they had been " waiting."
There was an instant response, and he had a large
nucleus already at hand for his Society. These
Seeker groups supplied an important band of
preachers, and they put Fox into contact with large
groups in other parts of the country. From this

time on the movement grew by leaps and bounds, and Fox saw the fulfilment of his hope becoming clearer every day.

He was surrounded by groups and individuals who were prone to be wild and chaotic. The small sects of the period, especially the Ranters, were enthusiastic and emotional. There are plenty of indications that he had to deal with many persons who had " complexes." He lived in an environment of intense dreams and hopes, and had to meet flattery and adulation enough to sweep a man off his feet. But the fact is, Fox steadily grew in judgment, poise, balance, insight and control. He became ever more robust and virile, and proved able to stand the brutal assaults of an unfriendly world, while he put through a schedule of labour and travel that would have broken down any ordinary constitution. William Penn could say : " I never saw him out of his place, or not a match for every service and occasion." He also says that Fox was " unwearied and undaunted."

All sorts and conditions of men came to regard him as a man to be respected. Cromwell instantly took his measure and knew that he had met an unusual person. Judges and gaolers were impressed by him ; so, too, were his fellow-prisoners. The students at Cambridge discovered that he had athletic prowess and could ride a horse as well as any of them. " I rid through them in the Lord's power, and they cried: 'He shines ; he glisters !'" Many testify to the piercing feature of his eyes, and no one can miss the magnetic character of his personality. He came to know the Light as a source of power, a unifying force, a stabilizing energy, and an underlying strength for his unresting soul.

Twice in his later life, once when he was thirty-five and then again when he was forty-six, he had serious recurrences of his nervous instability, and possibly there was a third instance, though that is not certain, while he was in Barbados in 1671. Both of the cases which he reports with some degree of fulness were occasioned by profound mental distress over the existing state of affairs, in the first instance in 1659, when he was deeply exercised over the state of the country, and the second time, in 1670, over the terrible suffering of Friends. Of the first recurrence he narrates : " While I was under some travail at Reading, by reason of grief and sorrow of mind, and the great exercise that was upon my spirit, my countenance was altered and I looked poor and thin." " And then having recovered and got through my travails and sufferings, my body and face swelled, when I came abroad into the air." [1]

The second instance involved a much profounder transformation and was more like the occurrences in his early agonies of search. I give the narrative greatly reduced and shortened : " Next day we passed toward Rochester. On the way, as I was walking down a hill, a great weight and oppression

[1] *Journal,* Eighth Edition, vol. i. p. 447.

fell upon my spirit ; I got on my horse again, but
the weight remained so that I could hardly ride.
At length we came to Rochester, but I was much
spent, being so *extremely laden and burdened with
the world's spirits*, that my life was oppressed
under them. I got with difficulty to Gravesend
and lay at an inn there ; but I could hardly eat
or sleep." Finally he got to Stratford, at the
home of a Friend named Williams. " Here," he
continues, " I lay exceedingly weak, and at last lost
both hearing and sight. Several Friends came to
me from London : and I told them ' that I should
be as a sign to such as would not see and such
as would not hear the truth.' In this condition I
continued some time. Several came about me ;
and though I could not see their persons, *I felt and
discerned their spirits*. Under great sufferings and
travails, sorrows and oppressions, I lay for several
weeks, whereby I was brought so low and weak in
body that few thought I could live. It was reported
both in London and in the country that I was
deceased ; but I felt the Lord's power inwardly
supporting me." A little later in retrospect he
says : " I was under great sufferings at this time,
beyond what I have words to declare. For 1 was
brought into the deep, and saw all the religions of
the world and the people that lived in them and
the priests that held them up." [1] Here we are
once more back under the *complex* of what he calls
" the world's spirits " and " the religions of the

world, the way people lived in them and the way priests held them up." For years his great constructive truth, his marching orders, had kept him unified and organized for his tasks, but worn out with labours, depressed over the suffering of Friends for the common cause, and weak in body and nerve, he falls once more under the old obsession and has a return of his disease. But underneath all his sense of suffering and of the weak and beggarly condition of religion in the world Fox still *felt the Lord's power inwardly supporting him,* and he evidently expected to come back into robustness of life again, as he eventually did.

This is the last sure sign of his mental instability, though his illness on the ship on the way out to America and the relapse in Barbados may have had some connection with the old trouble. Our first-hand intimate accounts of his life and experiences come to an end about this time, and we have only scrappy memoranda for the closing period, from 1675 to 1691, when he triumphantly cried, " I am clear." All his life through, and especially in the early period of it, he was staggered by the discrepancy between the religion of the Gospel and the religion of the Churches. This was the shaft which shattered his life in the period of his agony, and whenever he let the old " complex " master his mind he fell into disturbance and instability ; but for the most of his life a transcendent faith overmastered his fear—a faith that the Seed of God reigns. That was, in fact, his last message—

a triumphant message : " All is well ; the Seed of God reigns over all, and over death itself." This Seed of God for him means God revealed as the principle and power of a new and conquering life— God revealed in Christ and Christ revealed in a new spiritual body of men and women who reincarnate Him and propagate His Spirit. Nothing is better, after the storms and struggles of life, than to die, saying " the Seed of God reigns ! "

GEORGE FOX AS A PIONEER

By Elbert Russell, Ph.D.,
Professor of Biblical Literature in Swarthmore College.

A pioneer is a settler in new lands. He may not be the discoverer nor the first explorer of them. He is a leader of a new movement, though not necessarily its founder. Before George Fox's time many had already discovered the mystic way to God and had made ventures in group worship and spiritual brotherhood, and he entered into their labour. Indeed, he and his followers did not profess to have originated the Quaker ideal ; they claimed nothing more than that they were reviving " primitive Christianity." " Fox and Luther were parallel figures in so far as both of them were spokesmen of views and feelings that were widely entertained and in need of expression. This raises the question : How far was Fox original ? To what extent was his message his own ? If we adopt a common, though ridiculous, definition of originality, and claim that originality consists in saying and thinking what has never been said or thought before, then Fox was not original. Incidentally, no great personality in religion and ethics has ever been original in this sense, not even Jesus Himself." [1] An artist's work may be original, although he does not weave his own canvas ; an architect's, though he does not mould his own brick.

Fox's originality lies, first, in his principle of selection. He did not use all the material at hand. He adopted many Anabaptist ideas and practices, but he did not take over footwashing and women's prayer-caps. The Independents were pure congregationalists ; the Presbyterian policy was representative or republican ; Fox combined the two systems into a hierarchy of congregational meetings. The Ranters believed in immediate personal guidance, but rejected church government. Fox found the two not incompatible. The Seekers rejected existing forms of organized Christianity, but had found as yet none to take their place. Fox found a positive and satisfying substitute for the historic forms which he abandoned. Like a builder, he selected and shaped his materials into a purposeful and consistent unity. I do not mean to say that Fox was consciously eclectic, that he deliberately picked and chose among the sects. Rather, a new dynamic life rose in him, and it assimilated materials for its growing organism from contemporary religious life and thought, as a seed assimilates its food from the surrounding soil and air. He contributed an organizing experience and a dynamic personality.

[1] See H. G. Wood, *George Fox*, 1912, p. 132.

GEORGE FOX

In the second place, George Fox was original in making the " Inner Light " the sole and sufficient basis of personal life, religious belief, and of all forms of human co-operation, whether religious, political, or economic. The mystics of many groups through the Christian centuries had discovered this Divine Guide within men, but none of them had made it so consistently the sole basis of the whole life. Many had used it in limited relations, confining it to the individual or to the religious life or to the social organizations of small brotherhoods. Most of the historic mystics had in some measure abandoned or ignored the world or the Church or the State. George Fox trusted mysticism boldly as the basis of all departments of life.

In doing this he pressed the fundamental assumption of Protestantism to that logical and historic conclusion from which Luther and Calvin shrank back. He did not differ from them in claiming the right and acknowledging the duty of following his own inner leading for himself. Luther's faithfulness to his own conscience, to his ineradicable conviction that Tetzel was blasphemously wrong, led him to withstand popes, Duke Georges, and Diets alike. At the Diet of Worms he made it an ultimate principle : " Unless I am refuted by Scriptural testimonies or by clear arguments—for I believe neither the pope nor the councils alone, since it is clear that they have often erred and contradicted one another—I am bound by the passages of Scripture which I have cited, and my conscience is bound in the Word of God. I cannot and will not recant anything, since it is unsafe and dangerous to act against conscience." Calvin made the leading of the Spirit the basis of individual conduct and the ultimate basis of Scripture interpretation.

In practice, however, both great reformers were afraid to give others the same right. Luther dared not trust the " reason and conscience " of other men as the basis of the reconstruction of Europe. The Zwickau prophets, the Anabaptists of Münster, and the leaders of the Peasants' Wars did not follow Luther's light. He was afraid their liberty would mean the destruction of Church and State as they were, and he could not believe that the " Inner Light " untrammelled would serve as a trustworthy basis of their reconstruction. Calvin could trust the Spirit's leading only for the elect, and he could not believe that those who differed from him radically could be elect. When Servetus and Castellio disagreed with him as to the interpretation of Scripture, Calvin burned Servetus and hounded Castellio into exile and poverty.

The primary cause of their reluctance to apply universally a principle which they claimed for themselves was the ghost of Augustinianism, which still haunted Luther and Calvin. The shadow of the doctrine of Adamic depravity still lay upon their thinking. They could see nothing in man good enough and secure enough to be made the basis of a new order of human life. " Reason and conscience " were not reliable enough, nor the presence of the Spirit of God real enough to lead sincere minds to common conceptions of religious truth nor to serve as a basis of social co-operation.

The great contribution of Fox is that he believed that the divine manifestation in men is sufficiently real, objective, constant, and perceptible to form a reliable foundation for the whole of life. He trusted the inward guidance not only for himself, but for all. He dared trust it for personal salvation here and hereafter—as the fountain of religious belief and as the foundation of Church, State, and business. He broadened Luther's " reason and conscience " into the whole capacity of the human spirit for true conception of the one God in Whom " we live and move and have our being." He recognized the urge of the Holy Spirit in all men, saint or sinner, Papist or Protestant. He would deny God to no faculty of the soul. His " Inner Light " permeated every apartment of the inner man.

Many had conceived the possibility of human flight—Icarus, Darius Green, Langley—but the Wright brothers first showed the world a working model of a flying machine. Many had drawn up schemes of a world organization—Grotius, Penn, and Henry of Navarre—but the great contribution of Woodrow Wilson to internationalism is that he actually got a League of Nations going. So Fox gave a working demonstration of the saving suffi- ciency of the Inner Light in his own dynamic life.

AS A PIONEER

He created a working model of a mystical society.
He supplied the universal Spiritual Energy with
a human organization that actually did turn out
saints. In the midst of the most critical struggle
of this Society for existence under the Conventicle
Act of 1670 he sounded this note of victorious
faith in its fundamental principle :

My Dear Friends,
     The Seed is above all. In it walk ; in which ye all
have life.
     Be not amazed at the weather ; for always the just suffered by
the unjust, but the just had the dominion.
     All along ye may see, by faith the mountains were subdued ;
and the rage of the wicked, and his fiery darts, were quenched.
Though the waves and storms are high, yet your faith will keep
you so as to swim above them ; for they are but for a time, and
the Truth is without time. Therefore keep on the mountain of
holiness, ye who are led to it by the Light, where nothing shall hurt.
     Do not think that anything will outlast the Truth, which
standeth sure ; and is over that which is out of the Truth ;
for the good will overcome the evil ; the light, darkness ; the life,
death ; virtue, vice ; and righteousness, unrighteousness. The false
prophet cannot overcome the true ; but the true prophet, Christ,
will overcome all the false.
     So be faithful, and live in that which doth not think the time
long.   G. F.

As a consequence of his practical faith in the
Inner Light, George Fox pioneered in many lines
of religious reform and social innovation. It gave
him a new sense of the sacredness of human personality and of its reliability and importance as the
basis and goal of all human organizations. And he

identified the divine leading with the highest—with the altruistic and Christ-like—impulses in man.

It led him straight into religious democracy—inevitably, since all human beings as such have the same capacity for truth, virtue, and love, the same potentialities of divine sonship, the same immediate access to God ; since there is no respect of persons with God, and in the Christian fellowship " there can be no male and female " ; " there cannot be Greek and Jew, circumcision and uncircumcision, barbarian, Scythian, bondman, freeman ; but Christ is all and in all." Women were accorded by him full rights in worship and in the ministry of the religious Society he founded. They were given a share in the business of the Church, but, owing to the limitations of training and social custom, they were not at once admitted to that equal participation with men in the business meetings which has since been accorded them.

In the organization of the Society he secured wider connections than pure congregationalism affords ; he provided the means by which individuals and groups should have the benefit of the judgment and the co-operation of the larger groups in the Monthly, Quarterly, and Yearly Meetings, without sacrificing pure democracy. For the Monthly, Quarterly, and Yearly Meetings, while they correspond in gradation of scope and authority to Presbyterian session, synod, and general conference, are not merely meetings of appointed delegates of commissioners, but each is theoretically an assembly

of the whole constituent membership. His aim
was to secure a beneficent combination of individual
freedom with corporate counsel and responsibility.
He wrote in 1668 :

> For now, all coming to have a concern and care for God's
> honour and glory, that His name be not blasphemed, which they
> profess; and to see that all who profess the Truth walk in the
> Truth, in righteousness and in holiness, which becomes the house
> of God, and that all order their conversation aright, that they
> may see the salvation of God ; . . . that they may all see and
> know, possess and partake of, the government of Christ, of the
> increase of which there is to be no end.
>
> Thus the Lord's everlasting renown and praise are set up in every-
> one's heart that is faithful.

He recognized no limitations of caste or class
or race in religion. In the English meetings
master and servant worshipped together. He ap-
pealed to "that of God" in the Maryland Indians.
He urged the Barbados Friends to provide meetings and religious instruction for their negro slaves.
He wrote to American Friends :

> All Friends everywhere that have Indians or blacks, you are
> to preach the Gospel to them and to other servants, if you be
> true Christians.

Robinson, in his *History of Modern Missions*,
mentions Fox among the first Protestants to grasp
the idea of foreign missions. He became a pioneer
in the ideal of world-wide missions, because he
believed in the world-wide love of God for all
sorts and conditions of men and in the essentially
equal spiritual needs and capacities of all. He

wrote letters to the Pope, the Great Turk, Prester John, the people of Cathay, and printed an appeal " to all nations under heaven."

Fox was a pioneer in various efforts to " Christianize the social order." With the Puritans he was conscious that there was much paganism as well as " popish idolatry " in the historical churches— in their worship and in the amusements, literature, and ethics they tolerated or approved. But he went beyond them in the attempt to Christianize the common life. He would not call the months nor the days of the week by pagan names. He would have all days observed as holy days. He would not confine God to a " steeple house " for purposes of worship ; all places were sanctified by His presence.

I was to bring people off from Jewish ceremonies [he says in describing his mission], and from heathenish fables, and from men's inventions and windy doctrines, by which they blew the people about this way and the other way, from sect to sect ; and from all their beggarly rudiments, with their schools and colleges for making ministers of Christ—who are indeed ministers of their own making, but not of Christ's—and from all their images and crosses and sprinkling of infants, with all their holy-days (so-called) and all their vain traditions, which they had instituted since the Apostles' days, which the Lord's power was against.[1]

He would not conform to customs that put material values above spiritual, or placed selfish interests above those of humanity. He insisted that dress should not be a class uniform, marking

[1] *Journal* for 1648–9.

off " Cavalier " from " Roundhead," nor a means
of selfish display at the expense of the common
weal.   He would not deny the fundamental equality
of all classes of men by using the plural pronoun
" you " to single persons of so-called higher rank.
He was accustomed from childhood to take off
the hat in church during vocal prayer as an act of
reverence to God, and so refused to doff the hat to
men.   Many of these things seem to us trifling in
themselves ; they also seemed of small consequence
to Fox, except for the fact that the upper classes
attached great importance to them.   He says in his
Journal (1648–9) :

> Oh, the blows, punchings, beatings, and imprisonments that we
> underwent for not putting off our hats to men ! . . . Some had their
> hats violently plucked off and thrown away, so that they quite lost
> them.   The bad language and evil usage we received on this account
> are hard to be expressed, besides the danger we were sometimes in
> of losing our lives for this matter; and that by the great professors of
> Christianity, who thereby evinced that they were not true believers.
>
> And though it was but a small thing in the eye of man, yet a
> wonderful confusion it brought among all professors and priests ;
> but, blessed be the Lord, many came to see the vanity of that custom
> of putting off the hat to men, and felt the weight of Truth's testimony
> against it.

Fox insisted that the business of life should be
carried on honestly, truthfully, and humanely.   In
general, this would seem to be nothing more than
what the laws and the decalogue required.   But
Fox gave them new applications.   Oaths he would
not take, because they seemed to detract from the

obligation of truthful speaking at other times. Christians must " keep to Yea and Nay in all things."

The justices had the right in his time to fix the wages of farm labourers and servants. These magistrates were mostly of the landowning class, and the temptation was strong to fix a low rate. Fox frequently admonished the justices in person or by letter not to oppress the servants in their wages. At the same time he exhorted the servants to do their duty and serve honestly.

Trading in those days was regarded as more or less a contest of wits. It was the accepted economic theory down to Adam Smith that in a trade one party always got the worst of it. Fox often went to fairs to warn men against cozening in trade. He led Friends to adopt the practice of " one price to all," which put merchandizing on a more honest and fair basis. He tells in his *Journal* (1653–4) how Friends at first lost trade because of their religious and social " peculiarities " ; " but afterwards," he says, " when people came to have experience of Friends' honesty and faithfulness, and found that their "Yea" was Yea, and their "Nay" was Nay ; that they kept to a word in their dealings, and would not cozen and cheat, but that if a child were sent to their shops for anything, he was as well used as his parents would have been—then the lives and conversation of Friends did preach, and reached to the witness of God in the people."

George Fox was a pioneer in prison reform. This

was partly because he experienced the brutality
and cruelty of the prisons and gaolers personally.
He saw them from the inside with an outsider's
vision. It is not usual for conscientious, respectable, religious people actually to experience
the prisoner's lot, and it was partly because he
could not dissociate himself from the common lot
by moral complaisance nor theological doctrines.
It is common enough for people to complain
loudly of persecutions or abuses when they themselves are the victims, but complaisantly to persecute
or suffer others to be abused on the ground that
the latter deserve no consideration or mercy!
There was a subtle soul-poison in the current
doctrines of depravity and predestination. Men do
not try to be better than God. Since they believed
that He doomed all the non-elect to eternal torture
in hell, " regardless of human merit," why should
His devout worshippers worry if criminals, who
were certainly reprobate, fevered and rotted in cold,
dark, verminous, nasty, or stinking prisons? Fox
believed in the universality of God's love, in the
salvability of all men, in the sacredness of personality. He felt that even the criminal deserves
kindness at the hands of his brother-men, and
punishment should be for redemption, not for
torture.

His regard for humanity likewise led to opposition to capital punishment. Judicial murder was
abhorrent to all his God-given impulses. He was
particularly moved by meeting people sentenced to

death. He felt it to be monstrous that men should be hanged for so small an offence as stealing a sheep. Such a thing reversed moral situations and made the State seem the criminal and the criminal a victim of injustice and inhumanity. We find this record :

In this time of my imprisonment, I was exceedingly exercised about the proceedings of the judges and magistrates in their courts of judicature. I was moved to write to the judges concerning their putting men to death for cattle, and money, and small matters ; and to show them how contrary it was to the law of God in old time ; for I was under great suffering in my spirit because of it, and under the very sense of death ; but standing in the will of God, a heavenly breathing arose in my soul to the Lord. Then did I see the heavens opened, and I rejoiced, and gave glory to God. . . . Moreover I laid before the judges what a hurtful thing it was that prisoners should lie so long in jail ; showing how they learned wickedness one of another in talking of their bad deeds ; and therefore speedy justice should be done.[1]

Fox came into contact with negro slavery first in the Barbados in 1671. Thomas Clarkson says of him : " George Fox was probably the first person who publicly declared against this species of slavery, for nothing that could be deplored by humanity seems to have escaped his eye." [2] He was deeply stirred by it, though not at once ready to declare it to be inherently evil. He urged slave-holders to provide religious instruction for their slaves, to give them opportunities for meetings for

[1] *Journal* for 1650.   [2] T. Clarkson, *Portraiture of Quakerism.*

worship, and after a period of service to set them free, with provision for their old age. "He regarded the slave as a man, and plainly told the slave-holders that if they were in the condition of their slaves they would consider it ' very great bondage and cruelty.' " [1] The suggestion of the application of the Golden Rule to the case was definitely developed a little after by Edmundson. He wrote : " And Christ's command is to do to others as we would have them to do to us ; and which of you all would have the blacks or others to make you their slaves, without hope or expectation of freedom or liberty ? " After such an application of Jesus's principles, opposition to the system as essentially unchristian was inevitable. Pastorius and Woolman and Whittier did but develop and apply his pioneer suggestion.

More than one original idea carried out by his followers was first advanced by Fox. As early as 1660 he had the idea of a colony in America : Penn's first conception of it was in 1661. " We learn from a letter of Josiah Coale, a Friend who had travelled extensively among the Indians, that George Fox had commissioned him to treat with the Susquehanna Indians for the purchase of a strip of territory. Fox's letter is not preserved, but Josiah Coale's answer is among the *Swarthmore MSS*." [2] There can be no doubt that by this journey to America in 1671–3 the idea was revived

[1] R. H. Thomas, *History of Friends in America.*
[2] R. M. Jones, *George Fox : An Autobiography,* vol. ii. p. 515, note.

in Fox's mind and strengthened. He very probably conferred about it with Penn and the Quaker proprietors of the Jerseys on his return to England.

Fox's pacifist attitude was not a result of a reasoned conviction that war is evil. He underwent a religious experience that took out of him the motives that lead men to fight. At Derby they offered him a captaincy in a parliamentary regiment. If ever there was a righteous war or one for justifiable ends, this might have seemed such to him. The historic rights of Englishmen, liberty against the Stuart autocracy, parliamentary government, the supremacy of law, freedom of speech and Press, religious tolerance, Puritan morality and soberness against Cavalier wantonness and immorality—all seemed involved in the triumph of the " Roundhead " cause. But Fox records his answer thus : " I told them I knew from whence all wars arose, even from the lust, according to James's doctrine ; and that I lived in the virtue of that life and power that took away the occasion of all wars." [1]

Later, after the " Fifth Monarchy " uprising in 1662, he put forth with other Friends the following statement against wars and plots : " Our principle is and our practices have always been to seek peace and ensue it ; to follow after righteousness and the knowledge of God, seeking their good and welfare, and doing that which tends to the peace of all.

[1] *Journal* for 1650.

All bloody principles and practices we utterly deny ;
with all outward wars and strife and fighting with
outward weapons for any end or under any pretence
whatsoever : this is our testimony to the whole
world." He dared trust spiritual forces to order
and preserve human life and its value. He made
no exception as to self-defence ; nor would he
abandon public affairs in ascetic fashion, because he
could not, on the one hand, use military force, nor
believe it possible for the State to exist without it,
on the other ; nor did he feel the need of abandoning
his pacifist position to save the State in emergencies.
He believed that " the power of God " in men
furnishes a sufficient positive basis for the preservation of justice and the safeguarding of life and
property, and that the appeal to these is the true
ground of social progress.

Fox was a pioneer in recognizing the spirituality
and consequent universality of Christianity. In
interpreting the Bible, his spiritual insight often
led him aright against the letter of the text, and
in many cases it led him to anticipate the later
conclusions of critical scholarship. He could not
believe that anything outward could be of the
essence of religion ; holy days, consecrated buildings, sacraments, ceremonies, priesthoods could not
be essential, for as such they were limitations on
the completeness and universality of the soul's
access to God, and upon its communion, fellowship,
and service with Him.

Whilst I was under this spiritual suffering, the state of the New
Jerusalem which comes down out of heaven was opened to me;

which some carnal-minded people had looked upon to be like an outward city dropped out of the elements. . . . I saw that all who are within the Light of Christ, and in his faith, which he is the author of; and in the Spirit, the Holy Ghost, which Christ and the holy prophets and apostles were in ; and within the grace, and truth, and power of God, which are the walls of the city : I saw that such are within the city are members of it, and have right to eat of the Tree of Life.[1]

He could not share the millenarian views of many of his contemporaries because they involved an outward view of the kingdom of God.

On the spirituality of his conception of Christianity the testimony of Charles Spurgeon, the great Baptist preacher, is explicit :

George Fox . . . bequeathed to us in his last will and testament more than if he had given us the mines of Peru, for he has left to the Christian Church in the clearest and most unmistakable utterances a testimony for the spirituality of true religion. It is wonderful how full the testimony is. If you were to read through the lives of all the eminent saints, I believe you would come to the conclusion that of all others George Fox is the most distinct upon the one point, that " God is a Spirit, and they that worship him must worship him in spirit and in truth." [2]

Professor William James recognized that he was in these many ways the pioneer of modern liberal Protestantism : " The Quaker religion which he founded is something which it is impossible to overpraise. In a day of shams, it was a religion

[1] *Journal* for 1670.   [2] *Address on George Fox*, 1866.

of veracity rooted in spiritual inwardness, and a return to something more like the original Gospel truth than men had ever known in England. So far as our Christian sects to-day are evolving into liberality, they are simply reverting in essence to the position which Fox and the early Quakers so long ago assumed." 1

1 *The Varieties of Religious Experience.*

The Holborn Review, July, 1924.

THE STAND FOR PEACE

By MARGARET E. HIRST, M.A.,
Author of *The Quakers in Peace and War*, 1923.

Our forefathers and predecessors were raised to be a people in a time of great commotions, contests, and wars, begun and carried on for the vindication of religious and civil liberty, in which many of them were zealously engaged, when they received the knowledge of the truth ; but through the influence of the love of Christ in their minds they ceased from conferring with flesh and blood, and became obedient to the heavenly vision, in which they clearly saw that all wars and fightings proceeded from the spirit of this world, which is enmity with God, and that they must manifest themselves to be the followers of the Prince of Peace, by meekness, humility and patient sufferings.—Address of Philadelphia Yearly Meeting, 1774.

THERE is nothing in the early records of the Society to show that Fox and the other " publishers of Truth " acknowledged any influence from earlier sects in regard to the peace testimony. But Barclay, making a reasoned defence of Quakerism in the *Apology* (1676), points expressly to the " ancient Fathers " and " primitive Christians " as upholders of the unlawfulness of war, as well as, in his own time, to " others who with us do witness that the use of arms is unlawful to Christians." [1]

[1] *Apology*, Preposition XV, § xiii.

104

THE STAND FOR PEACE

For the first two centuries after Christ the Fathers condemned the soldiers' profession in unsparing terms, but a hundred years later, at the accession of Constantine, the official opposition of the Church to war had died away. It had been due, not merely to the pagan observances exacted from the Roman soldier, but to the essential nature of war. As the Church gave up the position, it was adopted by the heretical sects which, springing up in the East, overspread the Christian world. From the second to the seventeenth century there is an unbroken succession of these " heresies." Some are described as ascetics, Manichæans, practisers of unhallowed mysteries. Others were groups of earnest believers, drawn together to practise their interpretation of true Christianity. But the reported points of dissent from orthodoxy are curiously the same in all these sects. They tended to exalt the New Testament and belittle the Old, to reject or modify the distinction between priest and layman, and in some cases to reject also the ecclesiastical sacraments and ritual. They opposed war, military service, judicial oaths, and denied the right of the State to inflict capital punishment. Marcionites, Paulicians, Bogomili, Cathari, Albigenses, the early Waldenses, the early Tertiaries of the Franciscan Order (a " heresy " within the Church), some of the Lollards, the Bohemian Brethren (later Moravians), the Familists, and many groups of the first Baptists are links in the chain which stretches from Tertullian to Fox. In

his Seeker days Fox had much intercourse
with Baptists, and many of his early followers came
from that sect.

Quakerism is no isolated or sporadic religious phenomenon.
It is deeply rooted and embedded in a far wider movement . . .
a serious attempt to achieve a more complete Reformation, to
restore primitive Christianity and to change the basis of authority
from external things, of any sort whatever, to the interior life and
spirit of man.[1]

It is a strange misreading of Friends' principles
which charges them with too literal a reliance
upon certain passages of Scriptures. The words
of Fox are echoed by many other Friends of the
first generation. " These things I did not see by
the help of man nor by the letter, though they
are written in the letter, but I saw them in the light
of the Lord Jesus Christ and by His immediate
Spirit and power." [2] Hence the testimony against
wars and fighting arose from an inward conviction
that such practices were contrary to the Spirit of
Christ. The first recorded utterance of Fox on
the question was at Derby in 1650, when he refused
to win release from prison by accepting a commission in the new militia levies raised under the
Militia Act of July in that year, before the battle of
Worcester. " I told them I lived in the virtue of
that life and power that took away the occasion
of all wars. . . . I was come into the covenant of

[1] Rufus Jones, *Spiritual Reformers of Sixteenth and Seventeenth Centuries*, p. 348.
[2] *Journal*, Eighth Edition, vol. i. p. 36.

peace, which was before wars and strifes were."
His firm refusal earned him another six months of
prison, but he struck the keynote of the Quaker
testimony against war—the contradiction between
the spirit of war and the Spirit of Christ. Fighting,
like persecution, was the negation of Christianity.
"Take heed," he wrote to the magistrates who
imprisoned him, " of speaking of Christ in words,
and denying Him in life and power. O friends,
the imprisoning of my body is to satisfy your wills,
but take heed of giving way to your wills, for that
will hurt you."

Yet Fox obviously carried on no peace propaganda
among his fellow-prisoners, nor attempted to impose
his own convictions on them. The essence of early
Quakerism lay in freedom to follow the inward
guide, who would in due season lead the pilgrim
into all truth. Thus the "position" on war
came to be adopted at different times as an individual
conviction by the first members of the Society.
These included many soldiers or ex-soldiers—a
list of nearly a hundred can be made from scattered
allusions in contemporary writings. Not all left
the army at once, but it soon proved "impossible
for a Quaker to remain a soldier," [1] especially
after 1654, when Cromwell imposed an oath of
allegiance on the army. In the years 1654–7,
which was not a time of actual war, it was rather
the Quakers' opposition to oaths, titles, " hat-
honour " and their zeal for unauthorized preach-

[1] W. C. Braithwaite, *Beginnings of Quakerism.*

ing, which brought them into conflict with the authorities. Their views were thought subversive of discipline, and in 1657 a drastic " purge," both among officers and soldiers, was carried out. Besse, writing of the army in Ireland, says that many " came to be convinced of the truth gradually and . . . divers of them, as they became further enlightened, refused to bear arms any longer, and became able ministers of the truth, and publishers of the Gospel." [1]

In the navy, where Quaker principles were also making way, the convert had to face the dilemma of actual war. Thomas Lurting, in 1657, boatswain's mate of a frigate in the fleet attacking Spain, had for some time joined others of the crew in worship after Quaker fashion, when during a bombardment of Barcelona the thought came to him : " How, if now thou killest a man ? " He at once left his gun, though he did not then know that Quakers would not fight. But when he told his friends of his new conviction they united with him, remaining firm in face of threats till the ship reached England. Lurting entered the merchant service, in which once, when his ship was captured by Algerine pirates, he succeeded in taking the captors captive and landing them peacefully in their own country, without bloodshed or loss of life.[2]

---

[1] Besse, *Sufferings of the Quakers*, vol. ii., Ireland, 1656.
[2] Lurting's own narrative, *The Fighting Sailor turned Peaceable Christian*, 1710.

THE STAND FOR PEACE

At home the Militia Acts were a difficulty, especially after the Restoration. Heavy fines and distraints " for not sending a man to the militia " became a common " suffering." The first recorded instance is at Colchester in 1659, but it is almost certain that there were others earlier. Some were backsliders, like Thomas Ayrey, who " when like to suffer for truth's testimony against fighting and bearing outward arms, he consented to take arms," but most were as firm as Richard Robinson of Countersett " against bearing arms or finding a man for the militia, for he was all along charged with finding a man, but always stood very clear, and never after his convincement would pay anything directly or indirectly, but suffered for the same by fines and distresses, frequently encouraging other Friends to stand faithful." [1] In the uncertainties of 1659 some Friends were in doubt as to their position. Francis Gawler wrote to Fox from Cardiff, January, 1659–60, that Friends had been invited to enter a regiment of local militia and one had joined, " of whom we are tender, knowing he hath no bad end in it, but thinks he may be serviceable to truth in it." But the letter was endorsed by Fox, " Which G. F. forbade, and said it was contrary to our principles, for our weapons are spiritual and not carnal." [2]

---

[1] *First Publishers of Truth*, pp. 266 and 314. The quotations refer to dates after the Restoration.
[2] *Swarthmore MSS.*, vol. iv. p. 219 (in the Friends' Reference Library).

At the same time a constant suspicion of plots and conspiracy hung round Friends. The authorities often confused them with wild spirits such as the Fifth Monarchy Men. After the rising of these fanatics in January, 1660–1, thousands of Friends were flung into prison. The *Declaration* drawn up then by Fox and others was primarily to vindicate Friends of any share in the plot. " The Spirit of Christ," it declared, " by which we are guided, is not changeable, so as once to command us from a thing as evil, and again to move us unto it ; and we certainly know, and testify to the world, that the Spirit of Christ, which leads us into all truth, will never move us to fight and war against any man with outward weapons, neither for the Kingdom of Christ, nor for the kingdoms of this world. . . . Therefore we cannot learn war any more." Yet they suffered much during Charles II's reign under similar suspicions, as Fox's long imprisonments witnessed. In 1663 Francis Howgill assured Judge Twisden at Appleby Assizes : " If I had twenty lives I would engage them all that the body of the Quakers will never have any hand in war or things of that nature that tend to the hurt of others, and if any such, whom you repute to be Quakers, be found in such things, I do before the Court here and before all the people deny them : they are not of us." [1] Apart from

---

[1] Yet Howgill was imprisoned for life, dying in 1668. Besse, *Sufferings*, vol. ii, Westmorland. For these suspicions vide also *Extracts from State Papers relating to Friends.*

these suspicions, as the military system was re-organized, Friends inevitably came into conflict with its demands. A distinction, however, was made between war taxation and rendering military service or payments in lieu thereof. In 1659 Fox drew a distinction between bearing arms and " paying tribute " ; through the latter Friends " may better claim their liberty." Later he wrote : " So in this thing, so doing, we can plead with Cæsar, and plead with them that hath our custom and hath our tribute, if they seek to hinder us from our godly and peaceable life " ; whereas if payment were refused the Government might " plead against us, How can we defend you against foreign enemies, and protect everyone in their estates, and keep down thieves and murderers ? " [1]

The two volumes of Besse, and the records of many meetings, show long lists of distraint or imprisonment on account of the militia. In 1678 the Meeting for Sufferings requested returns of these as " a suffering for the Lord and His truth." In Kent Quarterly Meeting there are only fourteen years, between 1660 and 1702, in which there are no fines or imprisonments for this cause. Impressment on ships of war was also frequent, and the Meeting for Sufferings was much occupied in securing the release of victims. Well-known instances are those of Richard Seller, Thomas Lurting,

---

[1] Fox, *Epistles*, p. 137. *Swarthmore MSS.*, vol. vii. p. 165 (a paper on the Poll Tax of 1667 or 1678). In 1678 Sarah Fell paid £1 2s. in Poll Money for " father and mother " (George and Margaret Fox).

and Thomas Chalkley. Once a captain seriously tried to meet Lurting's scruples, as far as he understood them. Lurting told him he had been as great a fighter as others, but was now no more. "'I hear so,' said the captain, 'and that thou hadst a command, and so shalt thou have here; or else thou shalt stand by me, and I will call thee to do so and so; and this is not killing of a man, to haul a rope.' I answered, 'But I will not do that.' 'Then,' said he, 'thou shalt be with the coopers to hand beer for them, there is a great occasion for it.' I answered, 'But I will not do that.' Then,' said he again, 'I have an employment for thee which will be a great piece of charity, and a saving of men's lives—thou shalt be with the doctor, and when a man comes down that has lost a leg or an arm, to hold the man, while the doctor cuts it off. That is not killing men, but saving men's lives.' I answered, 'I am in thy hand, thou may'st do with me what thou pleasest.'" Seller, after winning recognition for his conscience, readily helped the wounded; Lurting would not accept an offer intended to enrol him in the ship's company for purposes of war.[1]

Perils from pirates and privateers led most merchants to arm their ships, and this difficulty also pressed on Friends. In 1690 a shipmaster connected with Friends at Liverpool armed his vessel. The Meeting for Sufferings reminded local

---

[1] For Seller vide Besse, vol. ii, Yorkshire. Lurting, *The Fighting Sailor*, etc.

Friends of the "ancient testimony. . . . It hath not been the practice of Friends to use or carry carnal weapons, and Friends at London have suffered much for refusing." In 1693 the Yearly Meeting Epistle rebukes some shipmasters who carry guns, "contrary to their former principle and practice . . . also giving occasion of more severe hardships to be inflicted on such Friends as are pressed into ships of war, who for conscience' sake cannot fight nor destroy men's lives." Therefore local meetings are asked "to deal with them in God's wisdom and tender love, to stir them up and awaken their consciences, that they may seriously consider how they injure their own souls in so doing, and what occasion they give to make the truth and Friends to suffer by their declension and acting contrary thereunto, through disobedience and unbelief."

During the cruel suppression of the Monmouth Rebellion in 1685 Friends fell under some suspicion, but the Clerk of the Western Assizes told the Quakers in Ilchester that "on enquiry made he found but two of us among nine hundred" rebel prisoners.[1] One of these, Thomas Please or Plaice, though he bore no arms, was active in the affairs of Monmouth's army, and thus had "*ipso facto* gone from truth, and rendered himself no true Quaker."[2] Two or three others were

---

[1] Letter of Somerset Friends to Meeting for Sufferings, August 1, 1685.

[2] Reply of Meeting for Sufferings, by George Whitehead, August 22nd.

" dealt with," and expressed penitence, tor such offences as selling horses to the army.

In the Irish Wars of 1688–91 the sufferings of Friends as non-combatants were very great, both from the two armies and the plunderers who followed in their wake. Those in the less harassed districts organized relief and shelter for their fellows driven from home. At Limerick, Dublin, and elsewhere Friends supplied the prisoners taken from William's army with food and clothing, " so that many of them said, when at liberty, if the Quakers had not been there they had been starved to death." Yet only four lost their lives by violence. Four others are known to have taken up arms. Three were officially stated to have acted " scandalous to the principles of truth by us professed, and our known practice since we were a people." The fourth, after serious and lengthy consideration, was told that he " could not be owned " by the Society.

Thus, through the changes of Government in the seventeenth century Friends steadily refused to join in civil commotion or rebellion, but rendered obedience to the *de facto* Government so far as it did not conflict with their religion and conscience. In April, 1696, the Meeting for Sufferings delivered an address to William III (with which the King declared himself well satisfied) explaining why Friends could not join a recently-formed Association to protect the King by force of arms. " Not out of any disaffection to the King or Government nor in opposition to his being declared rightful and lawful King of these realms, but purely because we cannot for conscience' sake fight, kill, or revenge, either for ourselves or for any man else."

Early Quaker writings dealing with this question fall into three classes. Some, accepting the soldiers' profession as a necessity of the time, appeal to the army of the Parliament to use its power on the side of righteousness. Others set forth " the life and power that takes away the occasion of wars." Others, again, explain and vindicate the Quaker standpoint against misrepresentation. In Fox's writings all these positions are found. In 1654, after one of his frequent arrests, he was told that Cromwell would be satisfied by a signed promise not to take arms against the existing Government. The response was a document of which the theological implications were sharply criticized in later times. For Cromwell the essential passage was that in which Fox proclaimed his mission " to stand a witness against all violence and against all the works of darkness, and to turn people from the darkness to the light, and from the occasion of the magistrates' sword. . . . With the carnal weapon I do not fight, but am from these things dead." [1] Here, as definitely as at Derby, Fox stated his abhorrence of all war and of the employment of violence for political or religious ends, but he now made the further claim that part of his mission was to bring others to the same peaceable

[1] *Journal*, Cambridge Edition, vol. i. pp. 161-5.

state. He did recognize, though within strict limits, the power of " the magistrates' sword " in preserving order within the State. In those days soldiers were often put on police duty, and in this paper Fox repeats to " soldiers that are put in that place " (of maintaining civil order) the advice of John the Baptist to the Roman soldiers maintaining order in Palestine.[1]

In 1659, amid the general fear of renewed civil war, Fox earnestly exhorted " all Friends everywhere " to keep out of plots and fighting. " Fighters are not of Christ's Kingdom, but are without Christ's Kingdom." " All such as pretend Christ Jesus and confess Him and yet run into the use of carnal weapons, wrestling with flesh and blood, throw away the spiritual weapons." [2] In that same year, however, Edward Burrough, George Fox the Younger, and an anonymous " F. G." (possibly George Fox himself) were writing tracts of advice to the army, acknowledging its past work as an instrument in God's hands.[3] " F. G." and Burrough even gave it another task—to suppress the Inquisitions of Spain and Rome. Yet both writers

---

[1] For similar advice vide *Swarthmore MSS.*, vol. ii, pp. 25 and 66.

[2] For these letters and similar ones of an earlier date vide *Cambridge Journal*, vol. i. p. 338. *Journal*, Eighth Edition, vol. i. pp. 448–51. *Epistles* (1698), pp. 11, 103, 108, 137, 145. *Swarthmore MSS.*, vol. ii. p. 95.

[3] The " F. G." tract is attributed to Fox in an old volume of pamphlets, mainly by him, in the Friends' Reference Library (*Tracts* 1 : 56). The passage referred to, however, is strikingly similar to that in Burrough, and the signature " F. G." is seldom used by Fox. Other points of internal evidence seem to make the identification doubtful.

also pointed to Christ, Who destroys "the kingdom of the devil and the ground of wars."

Burrough himself, in 1660, while admitting that some Quakers were formerly soldiers, added: " We are now better informed than once we were. For though we do now more than ever oppose oppression and seek after reformation, yet we do it not in that way of outward warring and fighting with carnal weapons and swords . . . never since we were a people." An undoubted tract by Fox of the same date rebuked those " who kill about religion." " Christ ends that law of the Jews which they thought they did God good service by . . . for they could not love enemies that killed them, neither can they that love enemies now kill them." [1]

Isaac Penington, another adviser of the army, sent out a tract from Aylesbury Gaol in 1661 which was a plea for the recognition of the Quaker's conscience, " who, by the peaceableness and love which God hath wrought in their spirits, and by that law of life, mercy, goodwill and forgiveness which God by His own finger hath written in their hearts, are taken off from fighting and cannot

[1] Burrough, *Works*, 1675, pp. 537–40. *Writings of George Fox the Younger*, 1665, pp. 12, 68–70, etc. For F. G., vide *Tracts* 1 : 56 (in the Friends' Reference Library). Burrough, *Works*, p. 671. George Fox, *A Word on Behalf of the King . . . Fear God and Honour the King* (*Tracts* 45 : 28, in the Friends' Reference Library). Fox says in his *Journal*, this tract " did much affect soldiers and most people." In 1655 Burrough wrote to the army in Ireland of the Light " that reproves you in secret of violence, and will teach you not to make war, but to preserve peace on the earth " (*Works*, p. 93).

use a weapon destructive to any creature." [1]   He argued that by the faithfulness of individuals the blessed state of universal peace would ultimately be attained, and the nation need not fear destruction from its enemies during transition.   " It is not for a nation (coming into the gospel life and principle) to take care beforehand how they shall be preserved, but the gospel will teach a nation (if they hearken to it) as well as a particular person to trust the Lord, and to wait on Him for preservation. . . . I speak not this against any magistrates or peoples defending themselves against foreign invasions, or making use of the sword to suppress the violent and evil-doers within their borders (for this the present state of things doth require, and a great blessing will attend the sword where it is borne uprightly to that end, and its use will be honourable ; and while there is need of a sword, the Lord will not suffer that government or those governors to want fitting instruments under them, for the managing thereof, who wait on him in his fear to have the edge of it rightly directed) : but yet there is a better state which the Lord hath already brought some into, and which nations are to expect and travel towards."   The sentence " I speak not this . . . rightly directed " is sometimes quoted without its context or any explanation of the aim of the tract, as a proof that the early Quakers were not opposed to war.

Space only allows a brief reference to two other

[1] Penington, *Works*. Somewhat spoken to a Weighty Question, etc.

early writers. William Smith, of Beesthorp, Notts, who suffered much imprisonment for the faith, published two tracts on the subject.[1] *A Right Dividing and a True Discerning, etc.* (1659), argued that the only lawful use of the sword is for the repression of crime. But to some "the use of the sword is not known, they are out of the place of a soldier, neither do know a soldier's place, which is under the state of a man, violently to kill and destroy each other and know not wherefore. . . . They return not to it again, they see a further thing, the end of that." But soldiers who incline to Friends' views must not be hasty, but consider "whether God hath set them there." In 1661, in Worcester Gaol, he wrote another peace tract inflamed with a glow of mystical fervour, which for beauty of thought and expression takes high rank in the literature of religious experience. It tells of the growth of the Royal Army, "whose banner is love and their weapons goodwill," and of the way of peace in which they are led by their Prince.[2]

In 1662 William Bayly, an ex-sea-captain, published a plain statement of the Quaker position.[3]

---

[1] Both are in his collected works, *Balm in Gilead,* 1675.

[2] *The Banner of Love under which the Royal Army is preserved and safely conducted. Being a clear and perfect way out of all wars and contentions ; with a short testimony unto the Way of Peace. Given forth by the edification and comfort of all that truly fear God. Written by the hand of one that bears goodwill to all men.*

[3] *A Brief Declaration to all the world from the innocent People of God called Quakers, of our principles and belief concerning plottings and fightings, etc.* (The Friends' Reference Library, Tracts 99: 36).

" We bear goodwill to all people upon earth " ; this principle " is not an opinion or judgment which may fail us . . . but the infallible ground and unchangeable foundation of our religion . . . to us it seemeth as impossible for us to be found in such things (plottings, fightings and violence) as for a good tree to bring forth evil fruit." With any reputed Quaker thus guilty the Society has " no fellowship or unity."

When Barclay published his *Apology* (1676) he could assert as a tenet of Friends that " it is not lawful for Christians to resist evil, or to war or fight in any case." He considered " Revenge and War an evil as opposite and contrary to the Spirit and doctrine of Christ as light to darkness. . . . Through contempt of the same [Christ's] law, the world is filled with violence, oppression, murders, ravishings of women and virgins, spoilings, depredations, burnings, devastations, and all manner of lasciviousness and cruelty." After quoting Matthew v. 38 to end, he continues : " It is as easy to reconcile the greatest contradictions as these laws of our Lord Jesus Christ with the wicked practices of war, for they are plainly inconsistent. . . . Nevertheless, because some, perhaps through inadvertency and by the force of custom and tradition, do transgress this command of Christ, I shall briefly show how much war doth contradict this precept and how much they are inconsistent with one another ; and consequently, that war is noways lawful to such as will be the disciples of

Christ." His well-known exposition need not be summarized here. In the course of it he says : "Almost all the modern sects live in the neglect and contempt of this law of Christ, and likewise oppress others, who in this agree not with them for conscience' sake towards God." To the plea, "the Scriptures and old Fathers did only prohibit private revenge, not the use of arms for the defence of our country, body, wives, children, and goods, when the magistrate commands it, seeing the magistrate ought to be obeyed : therefore, although it be not lawful for private men to do it themselves, nevertheless they are bound to do it at the command of the magistrate," he makes the following reply :

"If the magistrate be a true Christian or desires to be so, he ought himself, in the first place, to obey the command of the Master, saying, *Love your Enemies*, etc., and then he could not command us to kill them ; but if he be not a true Christian, then ought we to obey our Lord and King, Jesus Christ, whom he ought also to obey. . . . Lastly, as to what relates to this thing, since nothing seems more contrary to man's nature, and seeing that of all things the defence of one's self seems most tolerable, as it is most hard to men so it is the most perfect part of the Christian religion as that wherein the denial of self and entire confidence in God doth most appear ; and therefore Christ and His Apostles left us hereof a most perfect example. As to what relates to the present magistrates of the

Christian world, albeit we deny them not altogether the name of Christians, because of the public profession they make of Christ's Name, yet we may boldly affirm that they are far from the perfection of the Christian religion ; because in the state in which they are (as in many places before I have largely observed) they have not come to the pure dispensation of the Gospel. And therefore, while they are in that condition, we shall not say, That war, undertaken upon a just occasion, is altogether unlawful to them.

"For even as circumcision and the other ceremonies were for a season permitted to the Jews, not because they were either necessary of themselves, or lawful at that time, after the Resurrection of Christ, but because that Spirit was not yet raised up in them, whereby they could be delivered from such rudiments ; so the present confessors of the Christian Name, who are yet in the mixture, and not in the patient suffering Spirit, are not yet fitted for this form of Christianity, and therefore cannot be undefending themselves, until they attain that perfection. But for such whom Christ has brought hither, it is not lawful to defend themselves by arms, but they ought over all to trust to the Lord." "How men can love their enemies," he said elsewhere,[1] "and yet kill and destroy them, is more than I can reach ; but if it were so, such as rather suffer than do it, do surely more love them." In his treatise on "Universal Love" he

[1] R.B.'s *Apology . . . Vindicated*, 1679.

gives as a chief mark among Friends of this principle ("which necessarily supposeth and includes love to enemies ") their refusal to reconcile Christianity and war. In 1678 Barclay addressed an appeal to the plenipotentiaries at Nimeguen, negotiating terms of peace between Louis XIV and Holland and the numerous allies of each side.[1] " The ground " of war and its horrors, he tells them, " is the want of true Christianity " ; Christ Himself has been crucified afresh. He points to the power and effect of the " light of Jesus Christ " among Friends. " Many of them who were fighters, and even renowned for their skill and valour in warring, have come by the influence of this pure light to beat their swords into ploughshares. . . . And there are thousands whom God hath brought here already, who see to the end of all contention and strife and that for which the world contends, and albeit the devil be angry at them—because he knows they strike at the very root and foundation of his kingdom in men's hearts—by a patient enduring in the Spirit of Jesus, they do and shall overcome."

William Penn heartily agreed in this unflinching condemnation of war. And in his view the " horrible injustice " of the social system, with its sharp

[1] *An Epistle of Love and Friendly Advice to the Ambassadors of the several Princes of Europe met at Nimeguen . . . by R. Barclay, a Lover and Traveller for the Peace of Christendom.* Latin copies of the *Epistle* and the *Apology* were sent to each Ambassador.

divisions of wealth and poverty, was in almost equal contradiction to the will of God.[1] In his introduction to Fox's *Journal* he condensed the peace testimony into the phrase " not fighting, but suffering." His work in the foundation of Pennsylvania is dealt with later. Here it may be noted that the miseries of Europe through the wars of Louis XIV drew from him, and later from another Quaker, John Bellers, proposals for a " League to Enforce Peace " on the lines of the *Grand dessein* of Henri Quatre.[2] Both appeals were addressed, not to Quakers, but to the rulers and statesmen of the warring nations. Both provided for a Federal Parliament of nations to adjudicate in all disputes, and for a limitation of armaments, with a federal army and navy to enforce decisions against any rebel state which resorted to war. Yet neither writer believed that one State would thus withstand the united strength of Europe, and Bellers ended his pamphlet by praying God " to bless the Princes of Europe with the knowledge of Thyself . . . that the noise of war may be heard no more, and that Thy will may be done in earth, as it is in heaven."

In the West Indies—the first colony visited by

---

[1] Vide *No Cross, No Crown,* and *Fruits of Solitude,* vol. i. p. 53 ; vol. ii. pp. 221-35. For Penn's views on war see (in his *Works) No Cross. No Crown,* ch. viii, §§ 6, 7 ; ch. xx, § 1. *A Key . . . to distinguish the religion professed by the people called Quakers. Primitive Christianity Revived.* Prefaces to Fox's *Journal* and Barclay's *Truth Triumphant.*

[2] William Penn, *An Essay towards the Present and Future Peace of Europe,* 1693-4. John Bellers, *Some Reasons for a European State,* 1710.

Friends—they suffered under the Stuarts much harsh imprisonment and oppressive fines for their refusal to bear arms.[1] In 1660 the Barbardos Council gave this refusal as a chief " Reason " for a heavy law against them. One youth even died from brutal handling. Yet in 1674 the Quakers were still resolute : " We are resolved to fight under no other commander than the Lord Jesus Christ." In the other islands the same troubles arose. At Nevis in 1675 the authorities offered as a compromise to allow Friends to act as " watchers " unarmed. Fox sent a strong letter in favour of acceptance ; it was their duty, he said, to report invasion or attack to the magistrates, " who are to punish such things." [2] But two years later Friends were accused of persuading others not to bear arms. This they indignantly denied : " but if any are convinced of the Spirit of God in their own hearts, that fighting with any carnal weapon to the destroying of any man, although their greatest enemy, be sin, then to him it is sin, if he do it." After 1689 Quakers shared in the general toleration, but various economic causes drove most of them to the American mainland or to England during the eighteenth century. It was during a visit to the Barbados that Thomas Chalkley was asked : " If one came to kill you, would not you kill rather than be killed ? " and replied, " No ; so far as I know my own heart I had rather be killed than kill."

[1] See Besse, vol. ii, and *Col. State Papers* (America and West Indies).
[2] Fox, *Epistles*, pp. 363-8.

The reply, and the reasoning with which it was supported, converted the hearer to peace views.[1]

In Pennsylvania the founder's policy was to govern on principles which avoided all occasion of war, and the success of his just dealings with the Indian tribes was complete. As long as Penn's principles prevailed Indians and white men were at peace. But his province was held by grant from the Crown, and thus it was at times swept into the whirlpool of European politics. Penn never interfered with the raising of a volunteer force by the Governor from the non-Quaker population, but the first Militia Bill passed by the Assembly (with an exemption for conscientious objectors) was at the time of the French and Indian wars in 1755, nearly forty years after Penn's death. In 1709 he had sternly rebuked an unscrupulous Governor, Evans, for an attempt to fine Friends in the Delaware counties (which had a separate and non-Quaker Assembly) for not bearing arms. " A thing that touches my conscience as well as honour . . . that any Friends should not be secure and easy under me in those points that regard our very characteristics." [2] In 1689, when the deputy-governor first raised the question of a militia, the Quaker members of the Council refused to act in the matter, although " we would not tie others' hands." " The King of England knows the judgment of Quakers in this case before Governor

[1] Chalkley, *Works*, p. 207.
[2] Penn-Logan *Correspondence*, vol. ii. p. 220.

Penn had his patent. If we must be forced to it, I suppose we shall rather choose to suffer than do it, as we have done formerly." This was the opinion of Samuel Carpenter, who formerly in Barbados had endured heavy distraints for refusal to serve. In a similar dispute with Governor Thomas in 1739 the Assembly declared that " very many of the inhabitants of this province are of the people called Quakers, who, though they do not as the world is now circumstanced condemn the use of arms in others, yet are principled against it themselves." This seems to be the first time that any such formula was adopted to express the Quaker attitude ; it was repeated in the preamble to the Militia Bill of 1755, shortly before the Quaker members gave up their seats in the Assembly. In the interval they had progressed along the slippery path of compromise, frequently granting money " for the King's use," which was, in fact, applied for military purposes. After the death of Penn in 1718 the proprietorship was in non-Quaker hands.

" In Rhode Island Friends were in office for more than a century, the Governorship of the colony having been held by them during thirty-six terms. The Quaker administrators were in frequent difficulty on the question of war, both against the Dutch and the Indians. Faced with orders from the Home Government to arm the colony against the Dutch, and with the demand of the inhabitants (the majority of whom were not Friends) for protection against the Indians, they were constantly compelled to choose between giving up either their scruples or their office, and as a rule they chose the former alternative—leaving the actual responsibility for warlike measures as far as possible to others, and annulling them as soon as public opinion would permit." [1]   The constitution of the colony was based on " freedom of different consciences," and the officials, even when members of the Quaker minority, had no right to force their convictions on their fellow-citizens.   On the other hand, during the Dutch wars the Governor and Council passed in 1673 the first known Act for the relief of the conscientious objector, refusing " to compel their equal neighbours against their consciences to train and fight and to kill," but assigning to them civil duties, such as the care of the sick and aged and the guarding (unarmed) of valuable property. [2]

In New England and in the southern colonies Friends, amidst all their other suffering, did not escape those for refusing military service ; yet on the other hand both Chalkley and Story give striking instances of the safety of unarmed and defenceless Quakers during the worst of the Indian troubles.

Occasional records show that the early groups of Friends on the Continent suffered " for not bearing arms."   During the late seventeenth and

[1] Edward Grubb, *What is Quakerism ?* p. 142.
[2] *Rhode Island Colony Records*, vol. ii. p. 495.

early eighteenth centuries many Dutch and German Friends joined in the emigration to Pennsylvania ; those who remained, in the lack of support from England, mainly joined the Mennonites, another peace sect.

The foregoing brief summary may serve to show that from the early days of the Society the peace testimony has been held as an integral part of its religious belief and practice. It was not based merely on the recorded teaching of the New Testament, although in full harmony with this, but it grew inevitably out of the conception of the Inward Light, the divine spirit in the souls of men, that lighteth every man that cometh into the world. That spirit, the Spirit of Christ, which leads into all truth, could never, if faithfully followed, lead men into hatred, revenge, deceit, cruelty, bloodshed, devastation, and all the host of evils bound up in war. Nor could its followers destroy their fellow-men, children of the same Father, in each of whom there was a measure of the same Spirit. Nor, again, could the gloss of a theologian nor the command of rulers and magistrates stand against this inner conviction of the soul. The different testimonies were, to the early Friends, inter-related and all-essential to the practice of true religion. Barclay, writing of the two against oaths and against war, says :

There is so great a connection between these two precepts of Christ that as they were uttered and commanded by Him at one and the same time, so the same way they were received by men of all ages, not only in the first promulgation by the little number of the disciples, but also, after the Christians increased, in the first three hundred years. Even so in the apostasy, the one was not left and rejected without the other ; and now again in the restitution and renewed practice of the Eternal Gospel, they are acknowledged as eternal unchangeable laws, properly belonging to the evangelical state and perfection thereof, from which if any withdraw, he falls short of the perfection of a Christian man.

In words already quoted in part William Bayly declared that the peace testimony was " not an opinion or judgment which may fail us, or in which we may be mistaken or doubt, but the infallible ground and unchangeable foundation of our religion (that is to say) Christ Jesus the Lord, that Spirit, Divine nature or Way of Life, which God hath raised and renewed in us, in which we walk and in whom we delight to dwell."

Apart from the constant exposition in Epistles and other documents of the official bodies of Friends, the same testimony is borne by a host of individuals in the later generation of the Society. Thomas Chalkley, Thomas Story, John Bellers, John Woolman, Antony Benezet, William Allen, Stephen Grellet, Jonathan Dymond, Joseph Sturge, Robert Spence Watson, and Joshua Rowntree—these are only a few of the names that rise to memory in such a context. But more eloquent and convincing than any written or spoken word is the patient faithfulness of humble men and women who have lived unterrified in the midst of danger without resort to arms, and have undergone loss, imprisonment, shame, suffering, and death itself rather than forswear the principle of peace. The " conscientious objector " is no new phenomenon. In England, the West Indies, the American colonies, the United States, and Australasia, for two and a half centuries he has baffled all attempts at coercion, whether by legal penalties or brutal violence.

In the face of this record of profession and practice some would maintain that the peace testimony is a mere individual preference to be held or abandoned by Friends at their pleasure, or would even condemn it as a modern error thrust among our accepted beliefs. To the latter position the whole of this historical statement may be taken as a reply. Those who uphold the former bring forward two or three inconsistencies of statement among Early Friends, of which that of Isaac Penington, already quoted, is the most notable. (Penington, as has been explained, firmly maintained that Friends, owning obedience to the law of love, could not themselves bear arms or take part in war.) There are also the inconsistencies of action by Rhode Island and Pennsylvania Friends holding public positions in time of war, and the address of Yearly Meeting in 1746 congratulating George II on the defeat of the Jacobite Rebellion. The last is the solitary instance of *official* inconsistency in the records of London Yearly Meeting, and three years later the Meeting for Sufferings clearly identified itself with the peace views of Barclay's *Apology*. The fact that in various wars a greater or smaller number of Friends in England and America have abandoned the peace position is hardly relevant, for only in one case did the dissentients claim to represent the accepted doctrine of the Society, and these—the body of " Free Quakers " in the War of the Revolution—soon melted away. Up to the present time dissentient Friends in the United Kingdom have never made any serious effort to modify the Queries and the Discipline, on the not infrequent occasions of their revision, in the direction of a less emphatic pronouncement on peace. The section " Peace among the Nations " in the Book of Discipline has been, if anything, strengthened of late, while for nearly sixty years the Eighth Query has reminded Friends of the duty of faithfulness to the Christian testimony against all war.

It is sometimes suggested that in the last century Friends have shifted from the original ground of the testimony, and now base it rather on humanitarian and philanthropic arguments. No doubt the influences of the period of the Revolution and of Napoleon, from the diverse sources of evangelical Christianity and humanitarian philosophy, did largely affect the thought of Friends. But, from the earliest period, the two golden threads of love towards God and love towards man intermingle in the web of their belief and practice. There is much humanitarian sentiment in Barclay, much philanthropy in Bellers and Benezet. John Woolman combines a most purely spiritual basis for his condemnation of war with a most deeply humanitarian sympathy for those who sin or suffer in its toils.

On the other hand, the statements by which members of our Society in the European War explained to Tribunal or Court-martial their convictions and principles, lay their main emphasis on spiritual and religious considerations, so far as these can be separated from those of humanity and brotherly love. The same may be said of the Yearly Meeting Epistles issued during the war. The first Yearly Meeting, that of 1915, in one of its minutes, recalled the basis of the testimony : " It is not enough to be satisfied with a barren negative witness, a mere proclamation of non-resistance. We must search for a positive, vital, constructive message. Such a message—a message of supreme love—we find in the life and death of our Lord Jesus Christ. We find it in the doctrine of the indwelling Christ, that re-discovery of the early Friends, leading as it does to a recognition of the brotherhood of all men. Of this doctrine our testimony as to war and peace is a necessary outcome, and if we understand the doctrine aright, and follow it in its wide implications, we shall find that it calls to the peaceable spirit and the rule of love in all the broad and manifold relations of life."

Report to the All Friends' Conference, 1920.

THE MISSIONARY SPIRIT OF FOX

By ROBERT DAVIS

Christians do all in their power to spread the faith all over the world. Some of them accordingly make it the business of their life to wander, not only from city to city, but from township to township and village to village, in order to gain fresh converts for the Lord.—HARNACK, *Expansion of Christianity*, vol. i.

GEORGE FOX's *Journal* might be described as a traveller's diary, so full is it of journeyings to and fro in all parts of England and Wales, in Scotland and Ireland, in Holland, Germany and America. The purpose of this essay is not to describe these travels, but rather to attempt to catch the spirit which inspired Fox and his followers and to understand the principles by which they were guided and the message which they proclaimed.

From the time of his enlightenment in 1647 until a few days before his death in 1691 he was, apart from the eight periods of imprisonment and two prolonged stays at Swarthmoor Hall, almost continuously moving from place to place in the service of truth. In these days of comfortable and speedy travel and religious freedom it is difficult to imagine the labour, the sufferings, the weariness and the perils involved in the prosecution of such work in the seventeenth century. During the weeks following the month of December, 1651, George Fox, we are told, trudged with untiring energy over the East and North Ridings of Yorkshire, urged forward by the compelling force of his great message. Like his great forerunner, the first missionary-pioneer of the Christian Church, Fox knew the perils of the sea and the horrors of prison dungeons. He faced, too, the rage and fury of those who opposed his message, for, judged by the orthodox standards of the day, he was a heretic. Through all these trials he bore a brave, strong and loving spirit. In the words of Thomas Ellwood, " he was valiant for the truth, bold in asserting it, patient in suffering for it, unwearied in labouring in it, steady in his testimony to it ; immovable as a rock." What has been said of Fox might be said with equal truth of some of his followers.

We turn now to ask what was the driving force behind this movement for the publishing of truth. These Children of the Light (as they called themselves) were " under ·a necessity to express themselves," and the sense of necessity and urgency were the outcome of a deep personal experience of God in their own souls. Something had happened— something so transforming, so illuminating, so compelling that they could not help talking about it. They had found God for themselves ; what they had found others might find, for to all men was given some measure of the Light of Christ. " The

Lord opened to me by His invisible Power that every man was enlightened by the Divine Light of Christ." " I was sent," says Fox, " to turn people from darkness to the light, that they might receive Christ Jesus, for to as many as should receive Him in His light I saw that He would give power to become the sons of God. I was to direct people to the spirit." Again he says : " I have a message from the Lord as the Prophets and Apostles had."

And so it happened that Fox became the leader of a band of Publishers of Truth, who, amidst much political confusion and barren theological disputings, set forth with prophetic power the Christian message as a gospel of life and liberation. They challenged the prevailing hard, Calvinistic doctrine of God and cared nothing for theories *about* God, because they had a knowledge based on the direct experience of God in their own souls. Fox tells us that he knew God experimentally. The revelation of God came through Christ, who is a living Spirit. "Christ it was who had enlightened me, that gave me his light to believe in, and gave me hope, which is himself, revealed himself in me, and gave me his Spirit, and gave me his grace which I found sufficient in the deeps and in weakness." To Fox and his followers God was a living Spirit Who had entered into direct personal relationship with men. " I preached the truth amongst them " (to the soldiers in Carlisle Castle), " directing them to the Lord Jesus Christ to be their Teacher, and to the measure of His Spirit in themselves, by which they might be turned from the darkness to the light, and from the power of Satan unto God." It was an evangelical message, for Christ was the centre of their preaching.

Brief consideration must now be given to certain features of this early Quaker missionary movement. Fox and his followers felt it their duty to take every opportunity of spreading the Light. On one occasion Fox, on entering Carlisle, spoke his message to the Baptists in the abbey, to the garrison in the castle, to the people in the market, and finally to the magistrates and others in the cathedral. Again we are told that several meetings were appointed " in ye parish of Bolton, in ye County of Cumberland, sometimes upon ye hills without and sometimes in houses and barns, as it pleased ye Lord to make way for his Truth in ye hearts of his people." [1] This is further illustrated by what we are told about Dorothy Waugh, of Preston Patrick, who went to Carlisle and " declared truth in ye streets on a market-day," and about Gervase Benson and Thomas Taylor, who, with several other public labourers, had many meetings in Dent, " sometimes in fields and commons, and sometimes in houses."

In the year 1654 Fox tells us " the Lord moved upon the spirits of many, whom he had raised up, and sent forth to labour in his vineyard, to travel southwards, and spread themselves in the service

[1] Norman Penney, *First Publishers of Truth.*

of the gospel to the eastern, southern and western parts of the nation ; for above sixty ministers had the Lord raised up, and now sent abroad out of the North country, the sense of their service being very weighty upon me." These publishers of truth went forth, frequently two and two, as, for example, Howgill and Burrough, Camm and Audland, Wilkinson and Story, Stubbs and Caton, Dewsbury and Farnsworth. "They were for the most part young men in the prime of their ardour and strength, who would follow the movings of life rather than the counsels of prudence in shaping the new religious movement to which they had vowed their service." [1]

It is interesting to notice that Fox, while encouraging Friends who possessed the required gifts to go out and "thresh," enjoined upon other Friends to keep up their meetings. Diversity of gifts was recognized, but the sense of responsibility for the publishing of truth was to be shared by all. In one of his epistles, written in 1652, he writes : "And when there are any meetings in unbroken places, ye that go to minister to the world take not the whole meeting of Friends with you thither, to suffer with and by the world's spirit, but let Friends keep together and wait in their own meeting-place, so will the life (in the truth) be preserved and grow. And let three or four or six that are grown up and are strong (in the truth) go to such unbroken places, and thresh the heathenish nature,

[1] W. C. Braithwaite, *Beginnings of Quakerism.*

and there is true service for the Lord." The regular holding of meetings for "threshing" among the world is a distinctive feature of the early London work.

At the beginning of his ministry Fox speaks of his sense of Divine leading—"thus I travelled on in the Lord's service, as the Lord led me." And so it was throughout. The work was carried on under a sense of divine guidance. These early Friends were constantly in prayer together. "The more they found opportunity for waiting together, the more were they strengthened in their hope and faith, and holy resolutions were kindled to serve the Lord and declare His message by word and life." On one occasion Thomas Stubbs and William Dewsbury were together at Hunmanby, and "the next morning it was with Thomas Stubbs to part with William and go towards Beverley; so we sat down and were in prayer and supplication to the Lord much of the day; William labouring to strengthen Thomas and encourage him in exercise and service for the Lord till about the third hour in the afternoon; so the day being far spent, Thomas took leave, and departed towards Beverley. Then William and I [Thomas Thompson, of Skipsea] made ready for our journey towards Malton." In another place, we are told, Friends had "no settled or appointed meetings, but on the first dayes of the week it was the manner of some of us to goe to some town where were friendly people, and there sit together, and sometimes confer one with another of the dealings of the Lord with us."

As to the results of this work, the records speak again and again of hundreds being convinced of the Truth. For example, speaking of service in Cumberland in 1653, Fox says : " Many hundreds were convinced that day, received the Lord Jesus Christ and His teachings with gladness " ; and Francis Howgill, writing from London in 1654, remarks : " The wisdom and power of God hath been with us, and there are hundreds convinced." [1]

The following passage is taken from a letter written by Edward Burrough and Francis Howgill to Margaret Fell from London in 1655 :

> We have thus ordered it since we came—we get Friends on the First days to meet together in several places out of the rude multitude, etc.; and we two go to the great meeting-place which we have, which will hold a thousand people, which is always nearly filled, (there) to thresh among the world ; and we stay till twelve or one o'clock, and then pass away, the one to one place and the other to another place, where Friends are met in private ; and stay till four or five o'clock.

These meetings were characterized by great manifestations of spiritual power, and hundreds were convinced of the Truth. " At present," says Burrough and Howgill, " many come in daily to the acknowledgement of the Truth."

On another occasion Howgill says : " The wisdom and power of God hath been with us, and

[1] See John Barclay, *Letters of the Early Friends.*

there are hundreds convinced." Alexander Parker writes about the same time to Margaret Fell that he and Wm. Caton were at a meeting in Moorfields, where many Friends were : "A mighty power there is amongst them, and many tender hearts there are among them."

Reference must be made to the use of homes, for there are frequent allusions to this form of service. In the Yorkshire documents we read of Robert Barwick, of Kelke, who with his wife received the Truth, and "their house was made a Receptacle for Travelling ffriends for many years." Richard Robinson, of Countersett (Wensleydale), "gave up his house freely to receive ye messengers and servants of ye Lord, both for entertainment and to keep meetings."

A certain justice, John Crook, of Ampthill, a convert of William Dewsbury's, made his house a centre for Friends. A meeting held by Fox, at Ifield, in Sussex, at the house of Richard Bonwick, became the first settled meeting in the county. Such instances might be multiplied many times.

In the initial stages of the movement in Ireland, we are told the meetings were almost always held in private houses.

Allusion must also be made to the use of literature for the purpose of spreading their views. The activity of the early Friends in this direction was most remarkable. It is said that prior to 1715 over 4,269 publications were issued by Friends. Fox himself wrote some three hundred pamphlets.

George Whitehead also took a prominent part in this work. It was an age of controversy, and the polemics of the time were characterized by virulence and insobriety of speech. But they were the expression of a deep religious passion. Many of the pamphlets produced by Friends were written in reply to attacks made upon them. " No sooner was a book or a pamphlet issued containing reproachful statements respecting Friends than some answer made its appearance." The first book published by John Bunyan was directed against the Quakers. It is comforting to know that " the verbal violence in which Friends indulged as well as their opponents was singularly free both from the spirit of persecution and from the filth of private scandal."

Though subject always to the guidance of the divine Spirit, the work was not carried on in any haphazard fashion. There is evidence of plans for a systematic campaign. Methods of organization were not despised ; indeed, they were found to be necessary, and wise and statesmanlike plans were adopted. It is, however, important to emphasize the point that organization was subservient to the vital force of living concerns.

The chief towns and industries at that time were in the south. London had a population of half a million ; Bristol, with 30,000, was the largest seaport town ; and Norwich, with a similar population, was the largest manufacturing city. These three places became the chief centres of service for the publishers of truth, who in this respect may be compared to the leaders of the early Christian movement.

Again, we hear of a fund collected at Kendal for the spreading of truth so that Friends with limited financial resources might be set free to carry out their service. Margaret Fell took a leading part in the establishment, development, and administration of this fund. Out of it the frugal wants of the publishers of truth were supplied, and they were provided with the necessary outfit of clothing for their long and arduous journeyings.

This brief and inadequate sketch of the missionary activities of Fox and the early Friends may be sufficient to show that the Quakerism of those great formative days can best be described as a mighty spiritual movement. It was a splendid adventure for the advancement of truth. " During the whole period of the Protectorate the Quaker movement had the force of a tidal wave, and the Quaker influence filled the country like a rushing mighty wind." [1]

If Quakerism is to be a creative force in the twentieth century those who call themselves Quakers must think of the Society of Friends not in terms of organization, but in terms of a spiritual movement which exists to spread the Kingdom of God amongst men.

[1] Henry W. Clark, *History of English Nonconformity,* vol. i.

The Friend, July 11, 1924.

GEORGE FOX AS A SOCIAL REFORMER

By Edward Grubb, M.A.

THE three-hundredth anniversary of the birth, in the month of July, of George Fox, the founder of the Society of Friends, or Quakers, presents an opportunity of estimating the value to the world of his life and work. In this essay it is proposed to treat the subject from the social rather than from the strictly " religious " point of view, though Fox himself would have strongly dissented from drawing such a distinction. For him all life was one, and his endeavour to raise to a higher level the relations of men to one another was the direct outcome of his conception of the relation in which they stood to God.

Fox's discovery of a Divine " Light " or " Seed " in the souls of men—itself the result of an intense personal experience in which " an ocean of light " from God seemed to disperse the " ocean of darkness " into which the theologies of his day had brought him—was but a recovery of the Johannine conception of the " Word " or Logos which had " become flesh " in Jesus Christ. It necessarily carried with it the conviction that the true Light

" enlighteneth every man," that God has no favour-
ites. All men everywhere were, at least potentially,
recipients of the Light, if only they would turn to
it and obey it. No one could call another person
" common or unclean " ; no group of men could
claim privilege or ascendancy over others. Belief
in universal Brotherhood, which is a direct outcome
of the sense of the worth of man as man, taught
by Jesus in word and act, became once more dynamic
when it was based on the assurance of " universal
and saving light." Hence " philanthropy," if we
use the word in its true sense of the love of man,
became an essential feature of the Christian way
of living. Everything in existing institutions or
social arrangements which obstructed the shining
of the Light in men's souls—everything that
starved or stunted the growth of the Divine " Seed "
within them—was contrary to the will of God and
must be wrestled with and removed.

Consequently the " Children of the Light,"
and Fox in particular, without knowing or consciously intending it, became the most ardent social
reformers of their day. They had no thought-out
philosophy of human relations, no settled scheme
for the reform of the institutions of their time.
It was simply that whenever and wherever they
saw humanity oppressed and degraded, the Divine
image in men's souls distorted and disfigured, they
felt a burning sense of shame and an irresistible
impulse to set men free. At the very outset of
his public preaching Fox heard an inward call to

approach the justices at Mansfield (who were met to fix the rate of wages for their district under the Statute of Apprentices) with an exhortation to provide at least "a living wage." We know, from the writings of his contemporary Winstanley and others, that such a protest against oppression was urgently needed. In Cornwall he met with the inhuman practice of "wrecking" ships and plundering their cargoes, and issued a public denunciation against it. The savage penal code of the time, and the barbarous cruelty practised in the prisons, of which, in the days of persecution, Fox and his friends had ample experience, were among the abuses to which they often drew the attention of the authorities. The reform of prisons in the nineteenth century was largely due to the initiative of Fox's follower, Elizabeth Fry.

The evil practice of slavery, which after being almost eliminated from Christendom had once more disgraced it, owing to the discovery of the New World and of the possibility of exploiting its rich resources with the labour of negro slaves, shocked the sensitive soul of Fox as soon as he came into contact with it. In the island of Barbados, in 1671, he exhorted the slave-holders to treat their negroes well, to train them in the Christian religion, and as soon as possible to set them free. He does not seem to have discerned that slave-holding was wrong in itself ; but his companion, William Edmundson, soon began to declare that it was inconsistent with Christianity, and was promptly brought before the Governor on a charge of inciting the negroes to rebellion. It was, however, another century before the Society of Friends in the colonies of the West purged itself from the stain of slave-holding. Thanks mainly to the labours of John Woolman, it has the honour of being the first of the professedly Christian bodies to make the practice inconsistent with membership. And on this side of the Atlantic the followers of Fox became ardent supporters of Clarkson and Wilberforce in their long agitations against the Slave Trade and the legal status of slavery in the British colonies.

The " Testimony against War " is probably the best-known tenet of the Society of Friends ; and, like the protest against slavery, it is an inevitable outgrowth of the central principle of the Divine Light in men. For those who really believe that other men's bodies may indeed be " temples of the Holy Ghost " cannot destroy them ; they must strive to live in the spirit of their Master and to follow in His steps ; and it is His voice in their souls, not that of a military authority, to which alone they can promise final obedience. Fox himself seems never to have had any doubt that war was an impossible occupation for the Christian. In 1650, before he had attracted many followers, he was urged to become a captain in the Parliamentary Army. " But I told them," he says, " that I lived in the virtue of that life and power that takes away the occasion of all wars." In the years that followed a considerable number of soldiers joined the Quaker ranks, and Fox does not seem to have been in a hurry to get them out of the army. He evidently preferred to leave them to the teaching of the Spirit of Christ in themselves. But, before the Restoration in 1660, most of them had either left the army of their own accord or been turned out of it as not amenable to military discipline. Just after the Restoration a fierce persecution broke out against the Quakers, who were suspected of complicity with the "Fifth Monarchy men" in a plot against Charles II. They therefore issued an elaborate Declaration, which contains these words : "We utterly deny all outward wars and strife, and fightings with outward weapons, for any end, or under any pretence whatever ; this is our testimony to the whole world." That is unmistakable, and it states what has always been the official position of the Quaker body. What troubles it has brought them into, and what difficulties and inconsistencies there have been in the endeavour to live up to it, have been well told in a recent book, *The Quakers in Peace and War*, by Miss Margaret E. Hirst.

It was in the American colonies that the practicability of their peace principle was put to the severest test ; for there they were not, as they were in England, barred out by law and practice from sharing in the work of government. The Quakers stand apart from most of the mystical sects that had preceded them, by their willingness, if called to do so, to take part in political activity.

For them no aspect of life was to be common or unclean, and the work of government might be a legitimate field for Christian service. In 1672 Fox wrote to the Governor of Rhode Island, in words that might well be inscribed on the walls of every Parliament House : " Mind that of God within you. Stand for the good of your people. Take off all oppression : and set up justice over all." It was a problem not easily solved for Quaker rulers in those colonies to keep clear of responsibility for armed defence, when a majority of their people, not Quakers, demanded it, and when they themselves felt no freedom to force their own way of life on others who did not believe in it. What they usually did was to retain their official positions, but to leave warlike measures to be carried out by colleagues who had no scruples against them.

It was in Penn's colony of Pennsylvania that their principles won the most noteworthy success. From the first they treated the native Indians with scrupulous justice, as men of their own flesh and blood, and these Indians became their firm friends and supporters. For more than seventy years, while Penn's principles were maintained in practice, they were perfectly safe without any armed defence, while other colonists, armed to the teeth, suffered repeated raids and massacres. Then, on the outbreak of war with France, they were compelled to retire from the Government, and the " holy experiment " came to an end. While it lasted, it proved impressively the practicability of the Quaker way of life. That way is much more than " non-resistance " ; it involves the faith and courage to appeal to the Divine Light in the souls of men, even the most apparently hardened and degraded, and to believe that justice and goodwill can disarm the fiercest foe.

The Great War of 1914–18 and its terrible aftermath have provided further opportunities for proving the efficacy of moral forces to exorcize the spirit that produces war—and, it is to be hoped, eventually to rid the world of the nightmare that oppresses it. In the work of healing and restoration the Quakers have taken a not unworthy place ; and at the present time, in many of the European countries, the minds of men are open as never before to receive the message of a spiritual Christianity that is prepared to take the risk of living by the law of love and in the spirit of the Cross. The infusion of such a spirit into our international relations is perhaps the soul without which our League of Nations will be but a feeble body. And so the world may yet owe much to the faith and insight, the courage and obedience, with which, nearly three centuries ago, George Fox followed the Light.

The Nation and The Athenæum, June 28, 1924.

THE "JOURNAL" OF GEORGE FOX

By J. St. Loe Strachey

Books of piety are seldom great literature. But here is a book in which the lamp of religion burns with its brightest, clearest flame, and yet is inspired with the true sense of letters. Here is what John Milton, quoted by Dr. Rufus Jones, the writer of the Introduction, calls " the precious life-blood of a master spirit." Here is the story of the man who founded the noblest Christian Society in the world—the Society which has most in it of the spirit of Jesus. But, though allied thus to the first, and so the most primitive, form of Christianity, there is nothing about the religion of the Friends which is primitive in the weak or trivial sense. Here is the form and substance of a religion fit for modern and enlightened communities. Here is a mysticism which is not childish, ridiculous, or unscientific. George Fox, when he founded and set forth the Quaker faith, acted in obedience to the scientific instinct. With an unconscious, but none the less magnificent, pride he tells us: "I came to know God experimentally, and was as one who hath a key and doth open." As Dr. Rufus Jones well tells us, " he discovered that God is not above the sky, or at the end of a logical syllogism, but is a living spiritual presence revealed within the soul." He believed with absolute sincerity, and that belief was enough, that though only a hungering, thirsting man, he had been in the prèsence of God. He ate and drank like the rest of us, but " saw God also."

William Penn, the man who by nature and upbringing was so far from Fox, said well of him: "He acquitted himself like a man, a new and heavenly-minded man ; a divine and a naturalist, and all of God Almighty's making." Here was the truth. Fox has one of the most certain marks of greatness. He inspires and vivifies those who write about him. He was indeed an aristocrat of the soul. Wherever he appeared he was a leader, and whether it was his fellow-prisoners, or the judges, or the gaol-keepers, or the mob, or His Highness the Protector himself, he made men say and feel, " Never man spake like this man."

Such a man was Fox, and such a man needs no formal panegyric or laudation. Again, he needs very little interpretation, for his words still live. There springs from the text an influence, a peculiar grace so sublimated that it must touch all hearts. It does not matter how much we may disagree with portions of Fox's theology, or with his practice, or perhaps still more with his fierceness in regard to his enemies, for no one can pretend that here he attained to the full position of his Great Exemplar. Still, wherever there is a good man, whatever his creed, he will feel that Fox was one of the Knights of the Holy Spirit, one of those whose one bond is that they have kept themselves unspotted from the world. Socrates might have smiled, but would have loved him and honoured him. Marcus Aurelius would have found in him the noblest and best of Stoics. Confucius might have thought that he had too much zeal and too little order, but must have revered him. Ignatius Loyola would undoubtedly have burned him, but with true tears of sympathy. Augustine and St. Bernard would have seen in him a brother. Joan of Arc would at first have not understood his fierce hate of all war, but she would have been reconciled to what she at first thought an aberration had she known that, like Sir Thomas Browne, he " naturally loved a soldier." He and soldiers, as the *Journal* shows, again and again got together by a kind of natural affinity in opposition. Fox, who in many ways was an epitome of humanity, was indeed always dealing in contradictions. Among others, he was actually painted by Sir Peter Lely, and while sitting—sandwiched doubtless between Louise de Quérouaille and La Belle Hamilton—he evidently inspired the painter. The face portrayed shows the most extraordinary mixture of kindness and fierceness, gentleness and firmness. The forehead and the eyes belie the nose and the mouth, but the chin seems to give the balance to the hard side of the face. But perhaps it is not really strange that Lely should have painted him. One feels as one reads the *Journal* that Fox was far more at home and in sympathy with courtiers, soldiers, and worldly men than with those who superficially were so much nearer to him in doctrine and habit of life and yet were leagues apart. No doubt he found it a good deal easier to make an impression on a high-born Cavalier than on a Republican and Puritanical Major-General. The exception was Cromwell, who was undoubtedly much moved by Fox. But then Cromwell had in him two men—the mystic and the practical man of action—and the balance was pretty even between them. A very little more of the mystic might have made the Protector a colleague and co-worker with the first Quaker.

Before I say anything about the *Journal* itself, I am bound to notice the fact that the character sketch which William Penn wrote as a preface to the original edition of the *Journal of George Fox*, which was published in 1694—that is, very soon after his death—is a masterly piece of interpretative biography. It is intensely modern in tone, and there is not an analyst of the mind and the emotions living to-day, from Mr. Lytton Strachey to Mr. George Santayana, or from Mr. de la Mare to Mr. Hardy, who would not have been proud to have made the *animi figura* achieved by Penn. I take an example almost at random :

In 1652, he being in his usual retirement to the Lord upon a very high mountain, in some of the higher parts of Yorkshire, as I take it, his mind exercised towards the Lord, he had a vision of the great work of God in the earth, and of the way that he was to go forth to begin it. He saw people as thick as motes in the sun, that should in time be brought home to the Lord ; that there might be but one shepherd and one sheepfold in all the earth. There his eye was directed northward, beholding a great people that should receive him and his message in the parts. Upon this mountain he was moved of the Lord to sound forth His great and notable day, as if he had been in a great auditory, and from thence went north, as the Lord had shown him ; and in every place where he came, if not before he came to it, he had his particular exercise and service shown to him, so that the Lord was his leader indeed ; for it was not in vain that he travelled, God in most places sealing his commission with the convincement of some of all sorts, as well publicans as sober professors of religion.

The first thought of an English scholar who reads these words is : Had Fox or Penn ever read *The Vision of Piers Plowman ?* Is it possible or likely ? I confess that I am far too ignorant of seventeenth-century bibliography to be able to pronounce any opinion ; but, all the same, the speculation has a natural fascination. Better, however, for my immediate purpose of leading people to study Fox and not to dismiss him as a zealot or a mystic, are some of the admirable phrases used by William Penn to paint his dear George. This, for example :

He was a man that God endured with a clear and wonderful depth, a discerner of others' spirits, and very much a master of his own.

He goes on to add that, though Fox's words might sound uncouth to nice ears, " his matter was nevertheless very profound." The passage ends : "As man he was an original, being no man's copy."

Here is Penn's deeply moving description of Fox's praying :

But above all he excelled in prayer. The inwardness and weight of his spirit, the reverence and solemnity of his address and behaviour, and the fewness and fullness of his words, have often struck even strangers with admiration, as they used to reach others with consolation. The most awful, living, reverent frame I ever felt or beheld, I must say, was his in prayer. And truly it was a testimony he knew and lived nearer to the Lord than other men ; for they that know Him most will see most reason to approach Him with reverence and fear.

Next to it come some delightful personal touches. We are told that he was " neither touchy nor critical " ; but " so meek, contented, modest, easy, steady, tender, it was a pleasure to be in his company." " He exercized no authority but over evil, and that everywhere and in all ; but with love, compassion, and long-suffering. A most merciful man, as ready to forgive as unapt to take or give an offence." As a summing up, what could be better than the following ?—

For in all things he acquitted himself like a man, yea, a strong man, a new and heavenly-minded man ; a divine and a naturalist, and all of God Almighty's making. I have been surprised at his questions and answers in natural things ; that whilst he was ignorant of useless and sophistical science, he had in him the foundation of useful and commendable knowledge, and cherished it everywhere. Civil, beyond all forms of breeding, in his behaviour ; very temperate, eating little, and sleeping less, though a bulky person.

HIS "JOURNAL"

Penn, like a true, if unconscious, artist, ends :

I have done when I have left this short epitaph to his name :
" Many sons have done virtuously in this day, but dear George,
thou excellest them all."

It may seem strange that, admiring Fox as I
do, I have taken up so much of my space quoting
others and not Fox himself. Clearly to such an
accusation I must plead guilty ; but a good deal
might be said in my defence, and chiefly this—
that I am most anxious that my readers should
read and enjoy this memorable book for themselves.
Besides its deep and moving piety, it is full of
strange, curious, and attractive things—indeed, no
one can understand the great years from 1640 to
1690 without having read it. We are too apt to
think of that age as if it consisted of nothing but
Drydens and Halifaxes, Wycherleys and Miltons,
Cromwells and Charles I's, Marlboroughs and
Louis XIV's. Fox's diary shows us the other side.
Perhaps I can best illustrate the interest that the
general reader will find in the book by quoting
from the pencil notes which I have freely scattered
over my copy :
" Striking definition of religion.—Form of words
to act as substitute for an oath.—Lord Chief
Justice Hale.—The soldier's opinion of Fox (' He
is as stiff as a tree and as pure as a bell, for we
could never stir him ').—Account of his mother.—
Striking phrases.—Delightful and intriguing story
of the Sallee pirate which pursued Fox's ship on

his first voyage to America.—Charming correspondence with Princess Elizabeth, daughter of the
Queen of Bohemia.—Visions.—Account of dungeons.—Rude undergraduates.—Pictures of Cromwell.—Fox's legal ingenuity.—The Rape of the
Lock."

This last will, perhaps, raise my readers' curiosity
so much that it deserves to be satisfied. Fox in
the year 1687 was travelling in North Wales. As
will be seen, he did not altogether hit it off with the
fascinating Celts of those regions :

> Next day we passed thence into Flintshire, sounding the day
> of the Lord through the towns ; and came into Wrexham at night.
> Here many of Floyd's people came to us ; but very rude, and
> wild, and airy they were, and little sense of Truth they had : yet
> some were convinced in that town. Next morning there was a
> lady sent for me, who kept a preacher in her house. I went, but
> found both her and her preacher very light and airy ; too light
> to receive the weighty things of God. In her lightness she came
> and asked me if she could cut my hair ; but I was moved to
> reprove her, and bid her cut down the corruptions in herself with
> the Spirit of God. And afterwards in her frothy mind she made
> her boast that she came behind me and cut off the curl of my hair ;
> but she spake falsely.

The great passage about Fox galloping after
Cromwell's coach in Hyde Park and shouting
messages, spiritual and political, in through the
window is too well known for quotation. One
almost as good and far less well known is the
description of Cromwell sitting upon the table and
talking to Fox. It is, indeed, the most intimate

picture we have of the Protector and is to be specially cherished for his account, as well as Fox's. Fox describes how he and Edward Pyot went to Whitehall and spoke very seriously to Oliver Cromwell concerning the sufferings of the Friends. But this was not all. They, as Fox tells us, " directed him to the light of Christ, Who enlighteneth every man that cometh into the world." Then Fox proceeds :

He said it was a natural light; but we showed him the contrary, and manifested that it was divine and spiritual, proceeding from Christ, the spiritual and heavenly Man; and that which was called the life in Christ the Word, was called the light in us. The power of the Lord God arose in me, and I was moved in it to bid him lay down his crown at the feet of Jesus. Several times I spake to him to the same effect. Now I was standing by the table and he came and sate upon the table's side by me, and said he would be as high as I was; and so continued speaking against the light of Christ Jesus; and went away in a light manner. But the Lord's power came over him, so that when he came to his wife and other company, he said, " I never parted so from them before "; for he was judged in himself.

The whole passage may seem a little harsh and arrogant quoted in this way, but in its context it is not so. At the same time, Fox, no doubt, had a terrible tongue, and one can imagine a person who was not sympathetic to him often feeling deep resentment at his words and accusing him of having a viper's tongue. For example, here is the description of the way he handled the people at Edinburgh :

After this we returned to Edinburgh, where many thousands were gathered together, with abundance of priests among them, after burning a witch, and I was moved to declare the day of the Lord amongst them. When I had done, I went to our meeting, whither many rude people and Baptists came. The Baptists began to vaunt with their logic and syllogisms; but I was moved in the Lord's power to thrash their chaffy, light minds; and showed the people that, after the fallacious way of discoursing, they might make white seem black, and black white; as, that because a cock had two legs, and each of them had two legs, therefore they were all cocks. Thus they might turn anything into lightness and vanity; but it was not the way of Christ or His apostles to teach, speak, or reason after that manner. Hereupon those Baptists went their way, and after they were gone we had a blessed meeting in the Lord's power, which was over all.

Though Fox's magnificent courage, physical and moral, and the tongue which could lash men, not merely into fury, but into abject contrition, is again and again displayed in the *Journal*, no one can read the book as a whole without feeling that Penn was perfectly right in insisting on the mildness, gentleness, and humanity of the first and greatest of the Quakers.

The Spectator, August 16, 1924.

SHORTER ARTICLES AND
EXTRACTS

Dean Inge

THE little Society of Friends, the smallest of all Christian bodies, has just been celebrating at Kendal the tercentenary of the birth of its founder. George Fox was born at Fenny Drayton, in Leicester-shire, in July, 1624. In spite of the failure of Quakerism to attract either the classes or the masses—and numbers are a poor test of success in the things of the Spirit—Fox should rank among the greatest of religious leaders. The resemblance between his character and career and what we know of St. Paul is very striking. The Jews and Judaizers who plagued and persecuted St. Paul were very like the priests and " professors " who clapped George Fox into gaol, and shattered his splendid constitution by their cruelties. The mystical experiences of the two men were very similar, and both combined with the mystical temperament great gifts of organization. Fox's last words, " Now I am clear, I am fully clear," may be compared with, " I have fought the good fight, I have finished my course, I have kept the faith." The chief difference between them, as has been lately said, is that while with Fox it was his letters which were lumpy and ungrammatical, his bodily presence powerful and awe-inspiring, the opposite impression was made by the great Apostle of the Gentiles. St. Paul's conversations with Agrippa and Festus may be compared with the celebrated interview of Fox with Oliver Cromwell, which we should all have liked to hear. The conversion of the gaoler at Philippi was paralleled more than once in the life of Fox. Some of his gaolers joined the Society, and all were overcome by his dauntless courage and saintliness.

The Society which he founded has had its vicissitudes. The hopes of the first Quakers, that they had restored the primitive form of Christianity, which was destined to supersede Catholicism and Protestantism by reviving the fervour, the inwardness, and the democratic organization of the Apostolic Church, were disappointed. The Friends, after a brief period of rapid expansion, dwindled in numbers, and declined also in zeal. They became assimilated to the main body of Protestants, and accepted the main tenets of traditional orthodoxy, including reverence for the letter of Scripture. Thus they lost their main reason for existing as a separate body, and also the inner freedom of the mystic, which was their real strength. In America there was even disruption.

Latterly there has been a revival. The disintegration of Protestant dogma has recalled Quakers to the real strength of their original position, and the "Inner Light" has again come to the forefront in their preaching. The revival has been far more intellectual than the original Quaker teaching. George Fox was not a highly educated man, and there was an uncouthness about his sermons and the discipline which he imposed upon the Society which repelled scholars as well as men of the world. The external marks of Quakerism have now been dropped, though simplicity of dress and habits is still required. But the central doctrine of the Society is now pure mysticism, and several highly cultivated thinkers have recently joined the Friends from the Anglican Church and Nonconformity. The number of sympathizers is far greater than the number of adherents. Experiments in silent corporate worship have been introduced, after the Quaker model, by Canon Hepher and others, and have been much appreciated. Many Anglicans acknowledge deep obligation to Quaker devotional literature, but have no desire to cut themselves off from the sacramental system of the Church and from the appeals to the senses made by beautiful buildings, dignified ritual, and music.

But nothing has gained more respect for the Quakers than the events of the last ten years. The world is now nearly convinced that the Great War was a ghastly blunder, which ought never to have occurred. The witness of the Friends against militarism has been consistent and uncompromising. Without justifying those of them who refused to serve as soldiers, we must admit that a very difficult question of conscience was raised for them by conscription. And as soon as the call came, no longer to fight, but to repair the ravages of the conflict, the Quakers took the lead in relief work with extraordinary devotion and energy, combined with good sense and excellent business capacity. We never heard of a Quaker relief fund being mismanaged and frittered away, like certain others. The nations of Central Europe, in the throes of political and economic chaos, learned to bless the name of the English and American Quakers. They saw in them applied Christianity at its best, and judged the tree by its fruits. Considering the very small numbers of the Friends—about 150,000 in the whole world—their record in works of charity is amazing.

The future will show whether this remarkable sect is likely to grow in numbers, or whether it will be partially absorbed in larger bodies, which have made more accommodations to what the average man and woman mean by religion. There is much in Quaker theology, as now presented, which appeals to the thoughtful minds in our generation. Professor Rufus Jones, the able historian of the movement, sums up the foundational articles of the Quaker creed as follows : " The reality of God for us rests on the necessity to explain the time-transcending and space-transcending features of our own experience, the junction of the finite and the infinite, of time and eternity, within ourselves, and upon the fact that we cannot interpret any of our supreme values of life, like beauty, truth, love and goodness, without relating ourselves to a God in Whom we live, the life of our lives." This statement is quite free from the metaphysical dualism which left traces on some of the early Quakers, and sometimes threatened to make the " Inner Light " itself external. The Friends now have a sounder philosophy behind them ; and as long as they continue to bear witness to the truth of spiritual Christianity on the one hand, and on the other to the necessity and duty of combating strenuously the manifold evils of the world, they will point the way which the Churches ought to follow.

THE CHRISTIAN LIFE
July 5, 1924

THREE hundred years ago this month was born George Fox, destined to become at first notorious and then honoured for his stern and uncompromising maintenance of the right of private judgment. At a time when Episcopalians and Presbyterians were agreed, each in a different way, on the question of Uniformity, Fox found that " being bred at Oxford or Cambridge was not enough to fit and qualify men to be ministers of Christ." He therefore went forth to tell the Good News as it had been revealed to him, caring not whether his " meetings for worship " were assembled in churches ("steeple-houses," as he called them), in the market squares, in barns, or by the roadside. Persecution and imprisonment followed—as, indeed, it generally does follow all attempts " to turn the world upside down." Yet notwithstanding the efforts of the authorities, both legal and ecclesiastical, the disciples of George Fox remain to this day, smaller in numbers perhaps, but rich in influence in the affairs of our national life.

It was in the small hamlet of Drayton-in-the-Clay, or Fenny Drayton, in Leicestershire, that George Fox was born " in the month called July, 1624." His parents were godly folk, the father, Christopher Fox, a weaver, being nicknamed " Righteous Christer." Unlike the youthful years of John Bunyan, those of George Fox were not in any way remarkable for wrong-doing. From his earliest days he seems to have grieved whenever he heard quarrelling and angry words ; and while still in his teens men knew that when George said " Verily " nothing could shake his determination. In his twentieth year Fox was greatly troubled in

167

mind, not with any consciousness of wickedness, but with the temptations which assailed him on every side. "Temptations grew more and more," he wrote in later years, "and I was tempted almost to despair." The clergy to whom he confided his troubles could give him no help—one advised "a little blood-letting," another bade him "take tobacco and sing psalms"—but he found at this time the first promptings of his great mission.

The theology of that day held that men were born to suffer from the wiles of the Tempter, and to be for ever seeking forgiveness while striving to make their election sure. Against this doctrine the spirit of George Fox rebelled. He first questioned the reality of the temptations. Where do they come from, if they really exist ? Are we committed to a lifelong conflict with forces whose sole purpose seems to be to torture us ? Fox said " No " ; and, claiming that all receive from God a gift of the " Inner Light," he urged men everywhere to act according to the truth revealed to them, seeking always a fuller revelation from God. Once convinced of sin and accepting the voice within as a safe guide, all thought of fear for the future was banished. A man could then live in the new day and in the new light, feeling that he had been given a new and higher status in life. He was a being responsible only to his Maker, listening always to the voice of God speaking in his soul.

Against this new theory of salvation it is not surprising that the forms and ceremonies of the Anglicans, and the Calvinism of the Presbyterians, in turn ranged their forces. Fox and his followers were imprisoned. Yet they did not falter, and the persistence of their missionary spirit did much to wring from the authorities that freedom to worship and to manage their own affairs which has been for over two hundred years recognized—at least theoretically—as the birthright of the peoples of these islands.

Were it only for that reason, the name of George Fox should be remembered by all who love liberty ; and so to-day, somewhere near the three-hundredth anniversary of his birth, we are thankful to God that George Fox lived his life and accomplished the work to which he set his hand. He died on January 13, 1691, and was buried in the Quaker ground at Bunhill Fields. A long service in the Gracechurch Street Meeting-House preceded the scene at the graveside, where a crowd of some two thousand persons was addressed by William Penn, who had been the disciple and friend of Fox during his later years. Truly, as Carlyle has said " no greater thing was ever done than when George Fox went forth determined to find Truth for himself, and to battle for it against all superstition, bigotry, and intolerance."

THE CATHOLIC TIMES
July 12, 1924

NOT long ago was celebrated the Tercentenary of George Fox's birth, and an occasion is thus afforded for reviewing the position of the most interesting of all Protestant sects.

Interesting the Quakers certainly are. They stand at that fascinating point where extremes meet. The love of simplicity which made the earlier Puritans discard vestments and ceremony reached a stage among the Friends where it adopted a special garb and ritual of its own. With the exception of the Salvation Army, the Quakers are the only people among Dissenters who lend themselves to pictorial representation. No manufacturer of breakfast food would ever think of advertising his products as " Wesley Oats " or " Congregational Corn Flakes." These names are not sufficiently picturesque. They suggest no particular costume as a trade mark. It is left to the extreme wing of the anti-ritual army to provide this. The peculiarities of speech used by a previous generation of Friends, and still surviving here and there, is another indication of that love of outward form by which this body is distinguished from other Nonconformist societies. Among the stolid and prosperous modern representatives of George Fox's followers a faint flavour of romance still lingers, giving them a place in fiction which no Baptist or Presbyterian could for a moment obtain. The Quaker in fiction is a fairly familiar figure. It is a curious fate to have overtaken these simple folk with their homespun religion.

In addition to their association with these labels of speech and garb the Society of Friends lives in the public mind as a body of highly respectable citizens, industrious in business, active in philanthropy, and zealous on behalf of peace. It is strange that among these " marks " of " the True Quaker " is not to be found that special characteristic to foster which it might almost be said the Society was founded. The literature emanating from this body gives no evidence of a special acquaintance with " the Inner Light " of the soul. It is not to that quarter we look for guidance in the spiritual life. No member of this body has given us another *Imitation of Christ*, or even dared to enter the same field of heart-searching diagnosis as St. Augustine's *Confessions*. These classics of devotion were the work of men given over to the " externalism " of the Catholic Church. The special advocates of the spiritual and interior aspects of religion have nothing to give us to compare with the wisdom of St. Theresa's *Autobiography*. The Mary of contemplation appears to have developed into the bustling Martha of philanthropic activities. It would seem that the " Inner Light " tends to grow dim when divorced from the Sacraments of the Church. If the cultivation of the deeper life of the soul had been left to those who deny to it the sacred Food on which it is nourished where should we be now ? When we feel attracted by the quaint picturesqueness of Quakerism it is well to ask ourselves such questions as these. It prevents us slipping into the sentimentalism of modern " tolerance."

It would be easy to show that all the values which the Quakers are supposed to have made specially their own, and of which they claim to be the appointed guardians, have been developed far more fruitfully on the soil of Catholicism in conjunction with those elements which the Society of Friends repudiates.

No better illustration of this could be given than the movement known as that of the " Friends of God "—the nomenclature is significant—in the fourteenth century.

It was in the south of Germany that this movement arose. The times were evil. War ravaged the land. Famine increased the misery, and the climax of horror came when the Black Death broke out. In this time of suffering the Church was hampered by dissension. An interdict lay on Bavaria, and the ordinary means of grace were lacking to a people driven to despair by the calamities which Nature and their temporal rulers had brought upon them. The " Friends of God," under these circumstances, sought by mutual counsel to strengthen each other and to revive the spiritual life of those around them. "The Association they founded " (I quote from a Protestant source) " was kept secret lest through misconception of their principles they might fall under suspicion of heresy and the Inquisition should put a stop to their labours ; but they desired to keep themselves aloof from everything that savoured of heresy or disorder. On the contrary, they carefully observed all the precepts of the Church, and carried their obedience so far that many of their own number, even among the priests, were banished for obeying the Pope when the Emperor ordered them to disregard the interdict." Thus, under circumstances which cut them off involuntarily from the sacramental life of the Church, these mystics developed a mode of keeping alive the spiritual life not unlike that practised by the Quakers, teaching with as much sincerity and earnestness as they, the indwelling presence of the Holy Ghost. The times were such as to strain the loyalty of Catholic men and women almost to the breaking-point. Yet it was in no spirit of censorious isolation, such as one finds in the records of the early Friends, that they met to cultivate the inner life. They were not guilty, nor conscious, of any disloyalty in thus proclaiming the presence and guidance with the laity of the indwelling Spirit, and, when church doors were again thrown open, they flocked to renew their privileges as members of the Catholic body.

Quakerism has won a sentimental appreciation from numbers who would never think of becoming Quakers, but who welcome anything that looks like evidence of the possibility of nurturing the spiritual life independently of the Church. Mr. Bernard Shaw, for instance, has not escaped the temptation of representing Joan of Arc as a forerunner of George Fox. But Joan, like the " Friends of

God," nourished her soul on those Sacraments the validity of which every Quaker denies. If, in these cases, that simplicity of character and interior guidance supposed to be the special qualities of schismatics are found in their most highly developed types inseparably bound up with the sacramental life of the Catholic Church, what becomes of the argument for the necessity of schism as a means of giving freedom to the spiritual life from " the bondage of outward forms " ?

THE METHODIST TIMES
August 21, 1924

Rev. E. J. Ives

> Let us now praise famous men,
> And the fathers that begat us.
> The Lord manifested in them great glory,
> Even His mighty power from the beginning.

In any list of the pioneers of faith or of saints George Fox ought to have his place. Nonconformists have their calendar of saints as well as the Roman Church, and it is to their loss that the saints' days are not kept, in order to revive the witness that these men and women bore to their faith. We have but to remind ourselves of the debt Christ's Church owes to the Quakers, and to trace that mighty movement to its origin, to see at once what we owe to George Fox, whose tercentenary has just been commemorated.

Quakerism stands for so many elements of our common Christianity that we are apt to forget why the movement arose. It has emphasized the fact that religion is vital, experimental, dynamic; that religion must always express itself in social relations and in fellowship; that the Will of God is discoverable in corporate life as a corrective to individual interpretations of revelation; that in the silent and obedient waiting upon God His Spirit speaks to man and moulds their hearts to His desires; and that this communion with God is so real that men can dispense with creeds and ritual, seeing that they have Him who is " the creed of creeds " in their hearts as an Inward Teacher, and all life throbs with a sacramental significance. Every reader of history knows how Quakers have suffered, as pioneers always suffer. The doctrine of the " Inner Light " is liable to perversions; in essence it is what all Christendom at heart believes, even though many of us find Quaker practice makes too high a demand on the frailties of human nature.

THE GUARDIAN
July 11, 1924

ALL modern Christians are so largely in debt to the Society of
Friends for their steady assertion of the supremacy of conscience
that we ought not to allow the tercentenary of the birth of George
Fox to pass without a thought of the Leicestershire mystic, who
laid the foundation of a religious movement that has grown from
a few harassed groups of men and women in the seventeenth century
to the great and honoured denomination which the Society has
become to-day. " I came to know God experimentally," said
Fox ; and, from the moment when he first became conscious of
his spiritual mission, he was not to be deflected by scorn or con-
tumely from his life's purpose. His methods were doubtless
inconvenient to civil and ecclesiastical authorities in those unsettled
days, tending, as the old *mittimus* put it, " to the prejudice of the
reformed and established religion," and threatening " the publick
peace." But though he became acquainted with the inside of a
prison, and received some hard knocks in the course of his preachings,
this stout-hearted and saintly Englishman bent his back to no man,
and would never consent to barter his principles to save his skin.
" He acquitted himself like a strong man," wrote William Penn,
" a new and heavenly-minded man." And all Englishmen do
well to-day to honour his memory.

THE TABLET
July 12, 1924

As it is just three hundred years since the birth of George Fox, much is being said and written about this remarkable man and about the Society of Friends which he founded. While we join heartily in praising many philanthropic activities of George Fox's religious descendants, we cannot shut our eyes to the defects of the Society. If all Christendom turned Quaker, Christianity would soon be diluted into mere " social service," which is a vital part of true religion, but certainly not the whole of it. Modern Quakerism—we use the short word very respectfully—is like ivy : it requires the stout walls of historic Christianity for support, and its life would be a short one if it were cut loose.

Fox rediscovered the Light Within for his own time, reconstructed his religious system round it, and has made it a real power in England for three hundred years. More than any other man he made the Johannine interpretation of the Gospel into a practical religious system. . . .

He was oppressed by the moral impotence of Christianity in the presence of the wild forces of passion and destruction let loose in the war. The reaction from that experience was the discovery that he and his followers must live in the spirit which is opposed to all wars. No one has yet found a better way out of the ages of conflict into the ages of peace.

CHRONOLOGY

1624. Birth of George Fox (July).

1640. Beginning of Long Parliament.

1642. Beginning of Civil War.

1643. Fox's search for Light begins.

1647. Fox begins preaching.

1649. First imprisonment (Nottingham). Execution of Charles I.

1650. Second imprisonment (Derby, one year).

1651. Fox at Lichfield.

1652. Fox's vision on Pendle Hill. Wins the Westmorland Seekers. Visits Swarthmoor.

1653. Third imprisonment (Carlisle).

1655. Visits Oliver Cromwell.

1656. Fourth imprisonment (Launceston, eight months).

1657. Visits Wales and Scotland.

1658. Death of Oliver Cromwell.

1659. Publishes *The Great Mistery*.

1660. Restoration of Charles II. Fifth imprisonment (Lancaster, four months.)

1662. Sixth imprisonment (Leicester, a month). Quaker Act. Over 4,000 Friends in prison.

1663. Fox at Holker Hall.

1664. Seventh imprisonment (Lancaster and Scarborough, two and a half years).

1666–70. Fox settles meetings throughout England.

1669. Marriage with Margaret Fell. Visits Ireland.

1671–3. Visits America.

1672. Second Declaration of Indulgence. Persecution slackens.

1673–5. Eighth imprisonment (Worcester, fourteen months).

1675–7. First residence at Swarthmoor Hall (twenty-one months). Concludes his *Journal*.

1677. Visits Holland and Germany.

1678. Second residence at Swarthmoor (eighteen months).

1685. Death of Charles II. Accession of James II.

1688. The Revolution. Accession of William and Mary.

1689. Toleration Act.

1691. Death of Fox (January 13th).

1702. Death of Margaret Fox.

SELECT BIBLIOGRAPHY

WRITINGS.

The Great Mistery, 1659.
A Battle Door for Teachers, 1660.
The Arraignment of Popery, 1667.
A New England Firebrand Quenched, 1678.
Over 300 smaller works.
Journal, ed. by Thomas Ellwood, 1694.
Collected Works, 8 vols., 1831.
Journal, 2 vols., ed. Norman Penney, 1902. Friends' Bookshop.
George Fox, an Autobiography, ed. by Rufus M. Jones, 1904.
  Swarthmore Press.
Journal, 2 vols., 1911. *Short Journal*, 1924, ed. by Norman
  Penney. Cambridge University Press.
Journal, ed. by Norman Penney, 1924. Everyman Library,
  Dent.
Gleanings from George Fox, 1914; selected by Dorothy M.
  Richardson. Swarthmore Press.

BIOGRAPHIES, STUDIES, ETC.

A. Neave Brayshaw : *Personality of George Fox*, 1918. Swarth-
  more Press.
William C. Braithwaite : *Beginnings of Quakerism*, 1912. *Second
  Period of Quakerism*, 1919. Macmillan.
Thomas Hodgkin : *George Fox*, 1896. Methuen.
Rufus M. Jones : *Story of George Fox*, 1919 (for boys and girls).
  Macmillan. *The Life and Message of George Fox*, 1924.
  Macmillan.

GEORGE FOX

Rachel Knight : *Psychology of George Fox*, 1922. Swarthmore
Press.

Ernest E. Taylor : *Cameos from the Life of George Fox*, 1907.
Swarthmore Press.

Herbert G. Wood : *George Fox*, 1912. Swarthmore Press.